The Quantum Age of IT

Why everything you know about IT is about to change

The Quantum Age of IT

Why everything you know about IT is
about to change

CHARLES ARAUJO

IT Governance Publishing

Every possible effort has been made to ensure that the information contained in this book is accurate at the time of going to press, and the publisher and the author cannot accept responsibility for any errors or omissions, however caused. Any opinions expressed in this book are those of the author, not the publisher. Websites identified are for reference only, not endorsement, and any website visits are at the reader's own risk. No responsibility for loss or damage occasioned to any person acting, or refraining from action, as a result of the material in this publication can be accepted by the publisher or the author.

ITIL® is a registered trademark of the Cabinet Office.

First published in the United Kingdom in 2012
by IT Governance Publishing.
ISBN 978-1-84928-375-5

WHAT OTHERS ARE SAYING ABOUT THIS BOOK

The role of IT has changed in a revolutionary way. Success in this new world order will require a new way of thinking and a new set of competencies. Charles Araujo helps his readers understand the need for change as well as the ways that they must change in order to leverage this exciting opportunity.

Larry Bonfante, CIO USTA; Founder, CIO, Bench Coach, author, *Lessons in IT Transformation*

Araujo's easy-reading style belies the significance of his message. IT has changed fundamentally. Don't get left behind.

Mark Smalley, Ambassador at the not-for-profit ASL BiSL Foundation and freelance IT Management Consultant

Charles has really nailed it for any executive struggling with IT strategy. How IT got here and where it's going. This book really hits at the heart of what is missing in IT today and provides step-by-step approaches loaded with examples for steering the strategic course for IT in the 21st century. An easy read, yet will get the creative juices flowing for any IT professional executive!

Randy Steinberg, Author, *ITIL® Service Operation*, 2011 edition; Principal, Migration Technologies

A bracing indictment of IT dysfunction, and a well-informed discussion of promising avenues for IT improvement. I agree completely with Charlie that a systems approach is essential. Recommended!

Charles T. Betz, *erp4it.com*

What a great, insightful and thought-provoking work! The best part is that Charlie makes it practical and easily understandable with his real-life examples. Finally a road map for IT professionals who want to thrive in the business world into which they are being thrust.

Jaime Rosado Jr., Col. (ret), USAF, Medical Service Corps, FACHE, FAHM

It's courageous to start off a book about the future of IT by saying that IT as we know it is dead. As Charlie is careful to point out, however, IT didn't die overnight; it's been a long time coming. Taking a good look at the history of computing and information technology, Charlie shows us, step by step, why this is happening now, and explains why it is not necessarily a bad thing, and how a new IT business model is needed – and possible. Disruptions of the type we have recently seen in technology-driven businesses have shown that we need to make some hard choices. Those choices are clearly thought through and explained in detail in this book, taking into consideration various approaches to business discipline and to customer focus. Read this. Let's get on with it!

Roy Atkinson, service and support industry analyst and writer

IT has always been a complex journey, with unexpected twists and turns, but no road map. Guess what? Thanks to Charles, we finally have one. I highly recommend this book.

Frank Wander, Founder, IT Excellence Institute; LLC and Former CIO of Guardian Life

The goal of a CIO today is to see the future and enable their organizations to thrive in that new world. *The Quantum Age of IT* provides the insights to make that journey a successful one.

David Hummelberg, Senior VP, Solutions Delivery, the Capital Group Companies

Great! This is the most definitive book on IT transformation I have ever read. It clearly identifies how to perceive, treat, and integrate IT as a true business function, and stop treating it as a specialized staff function, the domain of techies and a money pit for most organizations. It should be required reading for all current and aspiring CIOs, CTOs and CISOs. This paradigm shift is happening right now and this book demystifies the steps needed to make the journey successful. Bravo!!

What Others Are Saying about This Book

Roman Hlutkowsky, Former SVP of Human Resources and VP of Operations Technology at FedEx Ground; Principal at the Hlutkowsky Group

With a clear and jargon-free approach, Mr. Araujo provides a compelling vision for a better IT organization and a road map for navigating the fundamental changes that are upon us. Leaders who are ready to forge ahead with a strategy that embraces this brave new world will be energized by these powerful ideas.

Michael Patterson, Ed.D., Adjunct Professor, Pepperdine University Graduate School of Education and Psychology; Co-author, *Have a Nice Conflict: How to Find Success and Satisfaction in the Most Unlikely Places*

This book combines the best of *The Fifth Discipline*, *Who Moved My Cheese?*, *Toyota Kata*, and *Chasing the Rabbit* for both IT executives and business executives alike. As Dr. Deming would say, survival isn't mandatory, so ignore it at your peril.

Gene Kim, founder of Tripwire, author of *The Visible Ops Handbook* and the upcoming books *The DevOps Cookbook* and *When IT Fails: A Business Novel*

FOREWORD

I met Charlie in early 2008 as part of a major IT transformational effort on Service Management I was leading at The Capital Group Companies, Inc. Although the practices of IT Infrastructure Library (ITIL®) and IT Service Management themselves weren't revolutionary, I realized that getting the IT team aligned in how these practices were going to be applied, and how we were going to deliver services differently to the enterprise was more about people than about tools and processes. It was critically important that I didn't underestimate the amount of organizational change leadership that would be needed to move the IT organization forward – giving up fragmented and numerous past processes, homegrown or massively customized tools used for Incident, Problem, Change, and Service Desk. I knew I needed outside help to get this done.

As a consultant, Charlie was quick to point out the magnitude of the challenge, and it was at that point, during the early days of our business relationship, that I saw something special in him. The way he thought, his approach, his almost defiant attitude towards the status quo, evangelizing the idea that this project wasn't just about technology, but about serving our business customers – creating a foundation of innovation that could drive higher levels of business enablement. It was really about *"The Quantum Age of IT"*.

As I began my initial reading of this manuscript, it was very clear to me that Charlie was onto something big … something profound … something IT professionals must not ignore. The notion that "IT as we knew it was dead, but we didn't know it" was more than intriguing, it was compelling. I had to read on, to find out why, and to learn what I was missing. In short, I needed answers.

From the first page, *The Quantum Age of IT* is a book that will resonate with anyone in IT, from those who are early in their careers to experienced veterans in the field. For me, it was a reflection of the undeniable changes taking place in the IT industry, game-changing events that simply could not be dismissed or ignored. They were bigger and potentially more disruptive than any others in the last 50 years, and they were coming incredibly fast!

"Objects in mirror are closer than they appear"

Beginning with his profound assertion that "IT as we know it is dead," Charlie proceeds to lay out the three game-changing shifts that have occurred since the early 1990s that have combined to fundamentally change the IT industry, the relationships we have with our business users, and the model in which we operate.

As I thought about it, I realized that deep inside I was instinctively aware of what was happening, but perhaps hoped that it was far off in the distance. Was I willing to accept that the future was now? As I reread the manuscript, the metaphor "Objects in mirror are closer than they appear" seemed to fit, and the changes that Charlie was laying out were coming faster and were much bigger than many of us might realize.

The dawn of empowerment had arrived, except that it wasn't about corporate IT. It was a game-changer for the business IT customer. The Consumerization-of-IT train had left the station, never to return. Suddenly, our business users had access to more powerful, and less expensive computing capability at home than they did at work. Corporate IT would no longer have the tight grasp or controls over the technology used by the business, which has the potential to render many IT workers irrelevant or, like dinosaurs, extinct.

In *The Quantum Age of IT*, Charlie begins with a brilliantly articulated and artfully organized review of the evolution of computing (presently known as IT), leading up to its death. He draws on the past to set the context for his vision of what future IT organizations will look like, comparing and contrasting two different, yet similar, organization models – Strategic Sourcer versus Strategic Innovator – arguing that both are strategic, but emphasizing the importance of picking the right one only after extensive discussions with our business customers.

Building on this foundation, Charlie follows with a description of the five critical traits every IT organization must develop and the five critical skills, or competencies, that all IT professionals need to posses in order to survive and succeed in the new Quantum Age of IT – none of which, by the way, are technical. Each is premised on the diminishing need for deep technology skills, offset by a growing demand for strong business skills. It's clear that the skills that got us here are NOT the skills that will get us to this new age of IT, to quote the book with a similar title from Marshall Goldsmith.

Using numerous examples, including a personal one involving his father, Charlie brings *The Quantum Age of IT* to life. With each chapter, he builds on his basic premise that IT as we know it today is dead, but holds up promise and excitement for what the new IT organization will look like and deliver, drawing on countless experts and noted author's insights to support his thesis.

Charlie concludes his book with a wealth of reference sources, tips and a "How-to" guide for getting started, including information on how to join the Quantum IT Consortium as a way to tap into and collaborate with others who are on a similar journey.

While conducting his work for me at Capital Group, I witnessed firsthand Charlie's mastery at applying these principles. Doing so with passion and inspiration, he instilled a mindset shift in my team that was truly remarkable. He introduced many of the ideas in this book, and then effectively wove them into our ITSM efforts as an overlay on the transformational changes that my team and I were able to deliver as a result of that program.

After observing his passion for organizational change and the manner in which he applied it, I recall thinking to myself: Somewhere there needs to be a book. A book that assembles his thought-provoking ideas – ideas that at the time seemed somewhat avant-garde or *nouveau* in how most people viewed IT. I felt there was a crying need to articulate the profound industry changes that were happening, and what the implications were for current IT organizations.

This is that book ...

Although written primarily with the IT executive in mind, Charlie's concepts and the vision that he paints for the new IT organization should be of interest to any IT professional.

As CEO and founder of the IT Transformation Institute and recognized expert in IT organizational change, this book gives Charlie the broader IT industry exposure he deserves.

Foreword

I am delighted to have played a small role by writing this foreword for his first book, but hopefully not his last.

An IT executive myself with over 25 years' experience, I've come across numerous books on IT that were nothing more than reporting on the latest fad, hypes, or new twists on old themes. *The Quantum Age of IT* isn't one of those; rather, it is a rare gem. To me, it should be on every IT professional's reading list.

Congratulations, Charlie!

Anthony Iorio

Senior Vice President, Information Technology Group

San Clemente, CA

ABOUT THE AUTHOR

Charles Araujo is the founder and CEO of the IT Transformation Institute, which is dedicated to helping IT leaders transform their teams into customer-focused, value-driven learning organizations. He is a recognized leader and expert in the areas of IT transformation and IT organizational change. He serves on the boards of itSMF USA and the Executive Next Practices Institute. He has been quoted in or published in magazines, blogs, and websites including ZDNet, IT Business Edge, ITSM Portal, TechRepublic, itSMF USA's Forum, *HDI SupportWorld* and *USA Today*. He is presently at work on two new books and speaks frequently on a wide range of subjects related to his vision of the future of IT.

ACKNOWLEDGMENTS

At some point, about halfway through the writing of this book, it occurred to me that I really could not pinpoint the exact moment that it had begun. I began formulating the specific concepts and structures presented in this book about a year ago, but the ideas began formulating long before. From conversations with clients who were willing to bring me into their inner circle, to industry experts who spent time with me talking about their views of the future, to the industry executives who graciously allowed me to interview them specifically for this book, this work is a reflection of countless conversations, shared insights, and heated debates. I am eternally grateful to everyone who has helped me, whether they realize it or not, and for the opportunity to be in the IT profession at what I believe to be such a profound and exciting time.

While I cannot thank everyone who has helped me, there are a number of people that I would like to specifically recognize for their contributions. Ron Pomplas, who is a senior IT executive at Avery Dennison, spent countless hours with me years ago as some of these ideas were first taking root. While I was a paid consultant, Ron's willingness to be open and frank with me provided me tremendous insights that have greatly influenced my work. In the same vein, Anthony Iorio, a senior executive at the Capital Group, took me into his confidence and let me see how he worked and how he achieved great results with his teams. Those experiences and insights were a great source of inspiration.

Acknowledgements

The ideas presented in this book came as a result of many late-night drinks, coffees, lunches, and other conversations. I cannot honestly count the number of hours that I had the opportunity to spend with great industry leaders exchanging ideas, debating and discussing the future of our profession. Those conversations unquestionably have influenced my work here. For the thought-provoking conversations, I would like to thank (in alphabetical order): Grace Bennett, Charlie Betz, Matthew Burrows, Shane Carlson, Evan Carlson, Tim Crawford, Chris Dancy, Shane Deay, Greg Downer, Paul Fitterer, Malcolm Fry, Mark Galligan, Ken Gonzalez, Dhiraj Gupta, Kelly Harrington, Joe Himelfarb, Matt Hooper, Bill Hough, Gene Kim, Rick Lemieux, Scott Leslie, Mark McCants, Steve Mejia, Ivanka Menken, Alex Munro, Susan Nunziata, Glenn O'Donnell, Simon Palmer, Leo Peay, Ravi Ramamurthy, Jason Rosenfeld, Aarti Shrikhande, George Spafford, Matt Terrones, Kathy Tito, Patrick von Schlag, Kurt Westphal, and Michael Woore.

I would like to thank the following reviewers for their helpful comments on the manuscript: Chris Evans, ITSM Specialist, and Antonio Velasco, CEO, Sinersys Technologies.

Special thanks and recognition are due to the IT executives who were gracious enough to allow me to interview them for this book. The ideas, experiences and views that they shared were instrumental in the development and support of these ideas. I would like to thank each of them for their willingness to share their vast expertise: Mojgan Lefebvre, Joel Manfredo, Joe Pleasant, Ashwin Rangan, Geoff Scott, and Bill Wray.

I would especially like to thank my two business partners, Jim Cross and John Palinkas. Without your steadfast support and encouragement, none of this would have been possible.

I also would like to thank the entire ITG Publishing Team, especially Angela Wilde, Vicki Utting, and John Gaunt, for their support and guidance.

Above all, I would like to thank my family. My father has been a true inspiration to me both in terms of the life he has led and in his never-ending belief in my ability to succeed and contribute. My mother is the one who taught me the value and power of love and of caring for others. You can see her fingerprints in almost every aspect of the personal advice I offer in this book. My children are the reason that I strive to contribute and to offer something of value to the world. I hope that I have made them proud. Finally, if it were not for my wife, this book would never have come to be. It has been, without doubt or question, her undying faith in me, her support and her partnership that has been the source of everything good in my life.

While I am very proud of this work, it stands on the shoulders of countless others. The people that I have acknowledged above, as well as the many authors and experts upon whose work I have drawn, have formed the foundation for this work. I believe that this book is a reflection of all that has come before. I hope that I have done justice to their ideas, insights and works and have added a small contribution to what has come before.

CONTENTS

Contents

Contents

Contents

INTRODUCTION

IT as we know it is dead.

That is a tough way to start out a book, but it must be said. If you do not believe it – or if you are not at least open to considering this as truth – you might just want to put this book down now. Everything that will follow is founded on this belief that everything that we know about IT is about to change – in fact, it already has.

Welcome to the Quantum Age of IT.

"Have you heard about this thing called the Internet?"

It seemed such an innocuous question. Idle chitchat.

"No." I answered. "What is that?"

It was 1990 and I was having an off-hand discussion with a client who worked for a large aerospace firm. Because of her ties to the defense industry, she had very early access to this new technology. She tried to explain it to me, but even though I had grown up in the 'modern' PC era, I could not quite grasp the concept. We chatted for a few more minutes and then moved on. I completely missed the significance of the moment. I did not realize that I had glimpsed the future. That I had seen, for a brief moment, something that would change everything.

Technologies come and go. They always have. How could we know that this one would be the one that changed everything? A lot of very smart people missed it. The reason is that we could not un-know what we already knew about how IT and technology were supposed to work. We could not escape the bias that this knowledge created. It made it nearly impossible to see the full ramifications of what this technology would bring.

It is called 'the Curse of Knowledge.' It was first illustrated in 1990, the same year as my glimpse into the future, by a Stanford graduate student named Elizabeth Newton.[1] In a series of experiments, she demonstrated that once we know something, that knowledge makes it nearly impossible for us to imagine not knowing it. This affects our ability to communicate and teach ideas because we assume that everyone else must also know what we already know. It also affects our ability to imagine alternatives to our current state. The curse of knowledge becomes a prison of sorts, trapping us in a perspective based on what we know to be true. Until, one day, it isn't true any longer.

It is why the vast majority of innovation during the Information Age came from outside the traditional technology domains. It was driven by people – 'kids,' mostly – who were not inhibited by the trappings of the old truths. They were not subject to the curse of knowledge, so they could imagine new futures that were simply outside the grasp of recognition of those of us who were living in the middle of our current reality. But just because we couldn't see it, that didn't mean that it wasn't happening. The transformation was happening whether we knew it or not – whether we accepted it or not. The new truth had been set in motion back in 1990 (and before) and what was

---

[1] The term 'the curse of knowledge' was first coined by Robin Hogarth in *The Behavioral Foundations of Economic Theory* (1986).

happening at the dawn of the Information Age was just the manifestation of this new truth.

We are at a similar point in time in IT organizations. The fundamental shifts in technology that began in the 1990s have now led to a fundamental shift in the organizational dynamics of the IT function within enterprises of all sizes. But the same 'curse of knowledge' threatens our ability as IT leaders to see this shift and imagine a fundamentally different future. There is a lot of talk about change and transformation in IT circles today. Most of this is not truly transformational – it is merely incremental. Incremental change will not be enough as we enter this new era for IT organizations.

* * *

This book has three primary goals. ***The first goal is to shake things up***. IT, as we know it, may be dead – but a lot of people do not know it yet. You might be one of them. You go through your day, facing the normal day-to-day challenges. You do your job and you try to do it well. You know that things are changing in IT (when are they not always changing, right?), but you are completely unaware that everything you think you know about your job, your career, your profession – everything – is changing right beneath your feet.

This is not your normal, run-of-the-mill change. This is big. This is game-changing. This is not a flavor of the month. The fundamental business model of the IT organization has changed and you need to understand it. This is so important that the first two parts of this book are dedicated to helping you see what is going on, convincing you that IT really is dead and to understand the IT business models that are rising in its place. You must see this new reality. You must understand the threat. And you must recognize what these new IT business models mean to your future.

Facing the death of your chosen profession is not a very pleasant thing. But here is the surprise. The death of IT as we know it is really not a bad thing at all. In fact, for those who see this for what it is and seize on it, this represents a tremendous opportunity. But how do you seize it?

The second goal of this book is to lay out the five organizational traits that will define the IT organization of the Quantum Age. In these five organizational traits is both hope and opportunity. These five traits represent the building blocks of the future IT organization. Within them, you will be able to define your future. What is interesting – and challenging – is that these five traits have very little to do with technology. These are not 'capabilities.' This is not about merely obtaining new technical skills. In fact, the term 'trait' is very purposeful. They represent the essential qualities that every IT organization must possess in the Quantum Age.

The five traits that every IT organization must develop and possess are that they must be:

- A Learning Organization
- A Disciplined Organization
- A Transparent Organization
- An Intimate Organization
- A Dynamic Organization.

You may feel that your organization already has some of these traits. You are probably right. That is the good news. Most organizations do. But they are often overshadowed by technical capabilities and are treated as 'soft capabilities' that are 'nice to have.' That is what has changed. These traits are the five characteristics that will define the success of an IT organization in the immediate future. Part III of the book will explain why these traits will now be at the center of how every IT organization operates; it will then break each of them down in detail. The goal is to help you understand these five traits and what they really represent. But knowledge is not enough. You must go in knowing that this understanding will come at a price. Once you understand it, you need to be prepared to act on it.

Which brings us to our third goal. There is nothing worse than knowing that things are changing, knowing that you are in a position to help lead that change, but lacking the skills to do it. Part IV of this book will outline exactly which skills you will need in the Quantum Age. You must be willing to accept that your most valuable assets will not be your technical skills. They will still be needed, but they will not be what provides the greatest value – either to you or to your customers. This part of the book will outline the five specific skills that you need to develop within yourself (and in those around you) to be a force of change, to be relevant to your customers and to take your place in the new IT business model.

Much like the five traits, the five skills that every IT professional needs to master are not technical. This is not about becoming a 'Cloud master' (or whatever the current buzzword might be by the time this book is published). But this is also not about a bunch of 'new age' soft skills. No meditation is required (although meditation is good!). In fact, the best way to describe these skills is that they are 'business skills.' In that, there is good news again. These skills will not be completely unfamiliar – it is just that they are downplayed and not spoken of often in IT organizations today. But that must change. The five skills of the Quantum IT Professional are:

- IT Financial Management Skills

- Critical Thinking and Analytical Skills

- Communication and Marketing Skills

- Innovation and Collaboration Skills

- Leadership Skills.

These five skills must be developed in abundance. They must permeate every level and every function of the IT organization. They are the foundational building blocks for developing the five organizational traits. And they will feel either foreign or like a complete waste of time to a large chunk of the IT organization. It is for those folks that this part of the book is written. *The third goal is to help you see that those technical skills that you have developed and honed over all of these years could well be your undoing, unless you are willing to recognize the changes that are occurring.* In these chapters you will see how this fundamental shift in the IT business model has led to a new set of needs – and how these five skills will help you meet them.

* * *

IT as we know it is dead. We are entering the Quantum Age of IT.

It is a time of great hope and opportunity for every IT professional who sees it for what it is. Will you?

Change is never easy. Especially fundamental change like this. It is our natural reaction to hunker down and try to weather the storm. From our experience with the constant stream of 'flavors-of-the-month' it is easy to take an attitude that 'this too shall pass.' But it won't.

The Quantum Age of IT is upon us. It represents a fundamental shift in everything we know about how IT organizations function and operate. There is no going back. This future will happen. *It is happening.* The only question is whether you will have this future merely 'happen to you' or whether you will lead this change forward.

For those who step up and lead their organizations, their teams and themselves into the Quantum Age, the future is bright. The Quantum Age does not represent a dark era for IT organizations. It represents a righting of the relationship between IT and its customers. It finally creates the relationship between IT and its customers that should always have existed. It ushers in an era of explosive growth in the application of technology to solve real and meaningful business problems – and to drive ever-increasing value for our customers. It offers an opportunity to make IT fun once more. A chance to finally move past the mundane to the strategic.

The journey into the Quantum Age of IT will be hard. There is no getting around that. A lot will be asked of you. You will be asked to learn new skills and to fundamentally change how you operate – and even how you think about your role.

But the journey will be worth it. At the end of this road is the IT organization that our customers have always wanted – the IT organization that we always wanted. One that is a fun place to work. One that provides consistent, meaningful and measurable value to your customers every day. One that is an engine for business growth and profit. One that not only can rapidly adapt to changing business needs, but also can help create competitive advantage. And one that does it all seamlessly and transparently, allowing our customers to focus on their business challenges and opportunities knowing and trusting that we are there with them every step of the way.

Welcome to the Quantum Age of IT.

PART I

IT IS DEAD

CHAPTER 1: THE HISTORY OF OUR DEATH (WHY THE MODERN IT STRUCTURE HAS FAILED US)

Jeff Winston was on the phone with his wife when he died.

First line from *Replay* by Ken Grimwood

The book *Replay* by Ken Grimwood is one of my favorite books of all time. It was a bit of a sci-fi cult classic when it was published in 1986. It was at once entertaining and profound. It tells the story of a man who dies suddenly at the age of 43 – only to wake up back in his freshman year of college. He learns that he has been given a great gift. A chance to live his adult life again. A 'do-over.' He decides that he will not make the same mistakes twice and lives his life differently. Until he reaches age 43 – and he dies again.

As this cycle repeats, he comes to a realization. He learns that changing his past is not the road to changing his future. He finds that his past experiences were a part of who he was and that spending his life looking backwards was only squandering the one thing of value that he really had – his future.

"The IT organization was in the middle of its next reorganization when it died."

Perhaps that should have been the opening line of this book. Much like Jeff Winston, we are at a similar point in the life of the modern IT organization. (As a happy coincidence, the modern IT organization is about 45 years old!). Our organizations have grown and evolved – in many cases, without much conscious thought. There was always too much work to be done to be contemplative. Sure, some strategic planning took place and there have always been the pundits and the prognosticators, but for the most part IT leaders were far too busy getting things done to waste time imagining their future. And, for the most part, it worked out just fine.

Then we died.

We just didn't know it.

But as Jeff Winston realized, this death is an amazing gift. It is an opportunity to give a fresh, new life to the organization. The lesson that Jeff Winston learned is the same one that we must now take to heart. There is nothing to be gained by complaining about our past or living in a world of 'what-ifs.' Our future lies in front of us, not behind us. But there are lessons for us in our past. There is clarity for our future to be found in the things that led us here. By understanding our past, we can better accept our today and then guide our tomorrow with an eye toward the future that we want to create. In order to envision our future, we must begin with the past.

The history of our death – part 1

How the function of IT came to be and the evolution of our organizational structure

The first computers were not computers at all.

The term 'computer' dates to the mid-18th century and literally referred to mathematicians whose job it was to perform long and arduous calculations by hand. They were typically hired by scientists to speed what would otherwise be a laborious process. Over time, the 'computers' realized the benefits of dividing their tasks and creating specialization. Eventually they created large books of 'premade' tables of already completed calculations so that greater calculations could be built from them. The first electronic computers were essentially created to replicate and replace the manual process that 'human computers' were performing. That fundamental process has continued to be the foundational drive behind all computing. To take what humans do slowly and imperfectly and enable it to be done rapidly and accurately.

By the time the modern mainframe computer was created in 1951,[2] this simple vision had spawned an entire industry, its own scientific discipline and, most importantly for our purposes, the beginnings of a new profession. By 1964, it was clear that there was a huge market for computers. But the complexity and cost of the technology made it difficult for most organizations to make the leap. It was into this market that IBM introduced the computer that would largely define the industry going forward, the IBM System/360 Series. It was a compatible series of computers that were all capable of running the same software. Based on this common architecture, it opened up vast possibilities for customers. The fact that it fit into IBM's existing infrastructure, combined with IBM's legendary sales force, suddenly made it practical and affordable for companies to begin purchasing the IBM System/360 Series and utilizing them for a wide range of purposes. As company executives began using their new technological marvels, however, they soon realized that they needed to employ a staff of people

---

[2] The UNIVAC 1 was developed in 1951 and delivered to the US Census Bureau in 1952.

who could program and operate them. And the function of IT was born.[3]

Technical foundations

From the very beginning, computers were set apart from 'normal' life. They were born in one of the greatest eras of technological advancement the world had ever seen. During the fifty years preceding the dawn of the commercial mainframe, we had been introduced to mass-produced cars, commercial air travel, and vast levels of 'automation' on both industrial and consumer levels. Everything from the automated assembly line to dishwashers, washing machines, and, of course, television had come on the scene in the short fifty-year period before the introduction of the commercial computer.

The world was in awe of technology. In 1955, Walt Disney inspired imaginations around the world with his new Tomorrowland area of Disneyland. In the 1950s and early 1960s there were over 150 movies released that dealt with the wonder of the modern era and imagined wild futures of flying cars and robots. It was into this world that the computer began its journey into the mainstream. It is no wonder that computers and the folks that operated them were viewed as something separate from the rest of the company.

The very first computers required highly technical people to design and implement them. They were advanced mathematicians and technicians who built and managed the entire platform. While the great innovation of the modern

---

[3] At the time, the function was often referred to as data processing.

mainframe computer was that it was 'programmable,' it still required a very technical skill set to write the binary code necessary to make it work. The work of writing this code was often long, arduous, and fraught with error. It was easy to make a simple mistake in the sometimes millions of lines of binary.

Companies, however, began to see the promise. They began imagining more diverse and more complex tasks that computers could handle. What started as a machine to do 'computations' was suddenly being used for a wide variety of purposes. With each new use imagined, the challenge of programming it became more acute.

Because of this complexity, two things happened. First, it became clear to organizations that the people that they needed to program and operate these new computers were going to be a special breed of people. This was not going to be something that just anyone could do. They would need to hire or train people with this specific skill set.

Second, the computer companies realized that they needed to do something. It was becoming apparent that, in some cases, it was taking longer to write the program to automate a task than it would have taken simply to do the task manually. So, they began developing 'programming languages' that made the job of programming a computer much easier. Languages such as FORTRAN and COBOL were introduced and represented the first major shift in how computing was done.

Specialization and separation

The creation of the first programming languages created a fundamental shift in how computers were used and operated. They opened up a world of possibilities for organizations by making it easier to do more complex and specialized tasks. This created an explosion in their use and was a boon for the growing computer industry. Suddenly, there was intense demand for programmers who could harness the power of these new investments.

The programming languages ushered another new aspect into the world of computing – specialization. Up to this point, computing was essentially a unidimensional discipline. The advent of programming languages and the large number of new computer companies that arose during this era brought with them a large number of subdisciplines specializing in specific platforms, programming languages, or industries. It was no longer enough just to be a programmer. Companies were looking for a "COBOL programmer on the DEC platform with experience programming financial systems."

This first level of specialization began creating divides. While at the beginning it was common for people to learn both FORTRAN and COBOL, over time people began to self-segregate. Scientifically oriented organizations were most interested in using their computers for complex calculations. The programmers were, therefore, predominately focused on FORTRAN because of its more advanced calculation capabilities. Business-oriented organizations concentrated on automating workflows and less complex calculations, so they focused on COBOL, which had been built to specifically meet this need. It became clear that there was not a great deal of crossover and so programmers began 'picking sides.'

This was not adversarial. Overall, IT people have always been collegial. It was more like the Tower of Babel. In the beginning we all spoke the same language. We could communicate, share stories, and trade roles. But over time, we began to forget. As programmers picked their sides and became specialized, they had little to no need for the other languages. So, we ended up working in different domains, speaking our different languages and working on different problems. Even within the same company this happened. If a company had a need for both technical computation and business-oriented computing, the two programming teams would self-segregate, each working on their own problems.

Soon, specialization became separation. Entirely separate camps of programming disciplines developed. They often involved different approaches, methodologies and documentation standards. The separation continued with the proliferation of additional computer makers, with each introducing its own separate set of parameters. What had begun as a singular approach to programming had evolved into a wide range of programming disciplines, each demanding different skills – and often different perspectives on how things should be done.

It was the first of many cultural divides to come.

The first silos

While programming skills were being internalized and stratified to meet the specific and increasingly unique needs of organizations, a separate discipline was developing elsewhere in the world of computing: the *computer operator*.

Originally, computers were operated in much the same way that the card tabulators had been operated before them. 'Programs' came in the form of punch cards and simply needed to be loaded in order to run the computer. The job was simple and was typically done by the same people that had put the old punch cards into the mechanical tabulators.

As computers became more intricate, however, this broke down. As they moved from punch cards to tape and from binary to programming languages, it became clear that the old way of operating the computer was not going to work. Companies realized that they had to hire people who could function in this new and specialized world and keep everything running. The role of the computer operator was born.

The division of labor was pretty simple and straightforward. The programmers wrote the programs and the operators operated the machines. They were fairly distinct disciplines and, while it may seem strange to us today, they had little dependency on one another. There was really nothing that operators could do to impact the programmers. As long as they ran the job, switched the tapes or whatever other operational task was required, whether or not the program ran correctly was solely in the hands of the programmer.

The same was largely true from the other direction. The operators did not much care what was in the program. There was little that the programmers could do that would have a major impact on the operators' ability to do the job. As long as they had sufficient instructions on the operational tasks required, the worst thing that could happen from their perspective was that the job would not run.

The discipline of computer operations was task-oriented. It was about executing a series of tasks consistently, reliably, and predictably. It was important work. But it was not one that required a high degree of creativity or ingenuity. A different type of person was attracted to the role of a computer operator. They were more mechanical. They were more task-oriented and enjoyed the idea that they were the guardians of the kingdom, making sure that everything worked as it was designed.

They also saw themselves as separate from the programmers. The divide continued.

The kingdom grows

Over the ensuing decades, this fundamental structure grew and expanded. New languages were added, new technologies were deployed, but everything ended up in one of these two 'silos.' In part, this was because the fundamental technology structure had not changed much. Improvements were made to the capabilities of specific components of the technology, making things faster or more efficient, but the basic architecture did not change.

Eventually, things like Project Management Offices (PMOs), security teams, and other ancillary functions were added to the IT operation. Sometimes this resulted in creating separate subfunctions within IT, but for the most part the two primary silos persisted.

After a time, these silos became fully entrenched. As IT grew from a technical discipline into a career, IT managers began to have a vested interest in this structure. Inertia set in. People were happy to keep things the way they were. After all, they seemed to work, right?

At no point did anyone really stop and ask if this was the right approach. IT and 'computing' were never seen as a strategic core competence during the early years. Viewed as largely technical functions, they did not warrant much strategic energy. They simply evolved.

The challenge was that it evolved based on a set of basic assumptions regarding the relationship between Applications and Infrastructure and between IT and its customers, who would themselves evolve over time, eventually leading to a fundamental break in these relationships.

The history of our death – part 2

The rise of the IT corporate culture and why we work the way we work

You can't win. You know that, don't you? It doesn't matter if you whip us, you'll still be where you were before, at the bottom. And we'll still be the lucky ones at the top with all the breaks. It doesn't matter. Greasers will still be Greasers and Socs will still be Socs. It doesn't matter.

From *The Outsiders*, by S.E. Hinton

The book and movie *The Outsiders* tells the story of two rival groups of teenagers locked in an age-old battle of cultural warfare. They come from different sides of the railroad tracks that physically and metaphorically divide those who have from those who have not.

The Socs (pronounced 'so-shus') come from educated and prosperous families. They are the 'thinkers.' They do not have to do manual labor. They will go off to college and, one day, they will be the boss. They see themselves as better than the rest.

The Greasers are working-class. They get their hands dirty. They are the ones that have to do the real work. They look at the Socs with disdain, living in their little world, oblivious to the reality of how things really get done. They see themselves as 'real' and the Socs as 'fakes' and pretenders who are blinded by fortune.

The separation between these two is clear. It is not just that they come from different backgrounds. They see themselves as different from one another. They cannot imagine that they have anything in common with one another. They each see their view as the right one – as the one that must be defended and protected.

The evolution of IT has led to our own version of the 'Socs' and the 'Greasers.' While there are no 'rumbles' going on in your typical IT organization, the cultural separation that has developed over the years is palpable. It may not be openly adversarial, but in most IT organizations the divide in worldviews and perspectives between 'Applications' and 'Infrastructure' is real.

It is not difficult to see why this occurred. But it is instructive to understand how this divide between the 'Socs' and 'Greasers' of IT developed and how it will impact IT organizations as the fundamental business model of IT shifts.

Different skills and different worldviews

The cultural wars that are playing out across IT organizations today started at the very beginning. The early computers were incredibly complex to design and build, but operating them was not.

Operating a computer involved loading some cards or loading a tape or invoking a few commands. Operators would monitor systems for jobs that did not run properly and either let the programmers know that they had failed or restart them if the error seemed environmental. Computer operation was mostly a manual function that required repeating many tasks over and over again.

Programming, on the other hand, was a sophisticated and nuanced activity that required a highly specialized skill set. It was the programmers who were the masters of the domain. Operators were the hired hands. Programmers were the translators between the business need and the code that would perform the needed function. They were equal parts architect and detective, designing and troubleshooting previously unimagined pieces of software.

As a result of these different skill set requirements, you could hire an unskilled person and train them to become an operator. That was much more difficult to do for programmers. A natural cultural divide, therefore, developed between the operators and the programmers. These were not equal, but separate, roles. But this was not as adversarial as it might sound or seem today. Both sides understood and accepted their role. If you were an operator, there was no shame in it. You had a job to do and you took pride in it.

It was really not much different to the relationship that existed during the dawn of the industrial age. There were engineers who designed and built and there were the machine operators in a factory who produced. It was the way things worked and everyone understood their role. This model worked in IT organizations for many years. The cultural divide was real, but it was not a source of stress. It just was.

Until, that is, something changed.

The rise of distributed computing changes the rules

The rise of distributed computing in the late 1970s and early 1980s changed the paradigm. The computer was no longer just a big box sitting in the basement that merely had to be operated. Suddenly, there was a 'network' of systems that had to be connected together in order to produce the desired result.

Up to this point, operators had just 'operated.' But as complexity fed into both specialization and separation, new operating platforms made up of multiple different systems had to be designed. It was no longer just operations. Creativity was required to design a system that comprised these various parts. While the role of operator would continue to exist, entirely new roles were being born to handle these new responsibilities.

As the complexity of IT operations expanded, new management and engineering roles were created. Unlike the simple operational roles of the past, these roles required much higher levels of skill and education and much greater interaction with the programmers. Systems were no longer islands unto themselves. Programmers were beginning to write programs that depended on environments outside their primary system platforms. This meant that the fundamental relationship in which programmers 'programmed' and operators 'operated' was breaking down. It was no longer that simple. Developing and executing an effective application now required that the two disciplines work together to design a system that would actually function.

There was only one problem: the cultural biases that had been formed at the beginning persisted. What had once been a simple paradigm was now fracturing. This began to create a significant amount of stress in the relationship between the programmers and what was now beginning to be called 'IT operations.'

Like the 'Socs' and the 'Greasers,' the two sides did not see eye-to-eye. The application teams continued to see themselves as the masters of the domain and did not fully understand the growing complexity of the infrastructure on which their applications ran. IT operations professionals, on the other hand, became frustrated that the programming teams did not give them credit for the work they did and for the complexity of their task, but also failed to realize the growing complexity that the application teams were dealing with at their end.

A future hindered by our past

As distributed computing rose and then gave way to the increasingly distributed and complex approaches that would follow, this complexity changed the fundamental relationship between the programmers (now mostly called 'application development') and the operators (now mostly called 'infrastructure operations').

The simple and clean model that had guided the early relationship – programmers 'program' and operators 'operate' – was woefully obsolete. Development could no longer be done in a vacuum. Server architecture, database design, and network architectures all could have a dramatic impact on application performance and even functionality.

In addition, as the applications themselves began to rely on increasing integration with other applications, the challenges multiplied. In many large organizations, it became common for no one in the organization to truly understand the full end-to-end design of a complex system.

It's different [from other engineering disciplines] in that we take on novel tasks every time. The number of times [civil engineers] make mistakes is very small. And at first you think, what's wrong with us? It's because it's like we're building the first skyscraper every time.

Bill Gates (Microsoft, 1992), from the documentary *The Machine That Changed the World*

This quote from Bill Gates was still from the early stages of distributed computing and before the explosion of the modern, Internet-driven economy that we know today. The situation has only become more complex. Every day, IT organizations are creating ever more complex systems that require intricate levels of integration to function properly. They span the disciplines of Infrastructure and Applications, but are hindered by the cultural artifacts of our roots.

The problem here is that the fundamental complexity of the systems demands a cultural posture of collaboration and mutual design. Application and Infrastructure teams, however, remain stubbornly rooted to their traditional worldviews. The 'Application Socs' do not want to be bothered with the infrastructure elements that may impact their applications. They want to be left to do their coding in peace. The 'Infrastructure Greasers' want only to remain focused on their technical domains, leaving business interactions and understanding to the application teams.

This is why to this day you will hear infrastructure teams gripe that they need 'dedicated windows' to complete their infrastructure changes – without having to coordinate with the hundreds of application teams that may be impacted. It is why you will hear application teams complain that the infrastructure guys should not be questioning or challenging anything about how the application is architected or developed – they should just stick to operations.

The Socs and the Greasers are alive and well. We are a victim of our past. We are a product of our roots. And while many have complained about it, it probably could have stayed this way forever. Except that something fundamental changed in 1999. Although no one realized it at the time, it would eventually lay bare the dysfunction of the internal IT organization and set the stage for the Quantum Age of IT.

Prelude to a change

Up to this point, there had been a constant evolution of technology, but the fundamental underpinnings of the way IT worked had not really changed. As new technologies had been adopted, new silos were created, but the fundamental building blocks of the organization, both structural and cultural, remained basically consistent. The cultural divide between Applications and Infrastructure had continued and grown and had pushed some IT organizations to the brink, but there was still little pressure to change the way IT organizations actually worked. Everyone complained about this cultural divide, but it was just the way the IT organization operated. The way it always had.

Then, in 1999, Google burst onto the scene.

Most did not recognize it for what it was. But it was the prelude to the fundamental shifts that were about to rapidly descend on IT organizations everywhere. It would take over ten years to fully materialize, but it would fundamentally change perceptions of how technology was supposed to work.

As people discovered Google, they discovered a power they had not known before. Suddenly, a world of information was open to them. All with the simplicity of a single search box.

Chapter 1 key points

IT as we know it is dead. It has happened gradually and right before our eyes. But this is not a bad thing. On the contrary, it represents a great opportunity. A gift. But only if we recognize it for what it is.

Here are the key points you should remember from this chapter:

- The IT function was never "created." It simply evolved as the new technology of computers burst onto the scene.
- As we evolved, we began separating ourselves into natural silos based on specialization (programmers versus operators) and platforms (e.g. COBOL versus Fortran).
- This eventually created a divided IT culture and a sort of Tower of Babel where entire teams within the IT organization no longer spoke the same 'language.'
- But as computing evolved and became more complex, the basis for this cultural divide broke down, fractured

and became a source of great frustration where the cultural norms that existed were in conflict with reality.

- While most recognized these cultural divides and silos, it might have remained unchanged except that something happened that would change everything.

CHAPTER 2: CONSUMERIZATION, CLOUDS AND A CHANGE IN PERSPECTIVE

In just one year, *Angry Birds* has sold over twenty million downloads. According to *Wired* magazine, it is the best-selling paid app of all time and has resulted in over three trillion pigs being 'popped.' It is the definition of an overnight success.

Except that it isn't.

Rovio, the Finnish developer of *Angry Birds*, was formed in 2003 and was on the verge of bankruptcy before their smash success. The road to their success began with a realization that gaming was becoming the new primary form of entertainment. The rise of mobile gaming subsequently offered a new path for the company. Then the release of the iPhone and its App Store in 2007 changed the distribution paradigm. Finally, Mikael and Niklas Hed, the company's founders, realized that the iPhone had changed something else. They saw that the market for mobile games was no longer gamers – that it had become *everyone*. That changed the rules about what would sell and how it would sell, so they set out to create a new kind of mobile game using a new set of parameters. The rest, as they say, is history.

An overnight success rarely happens overnight. What looks like a spontaneous rising was actually the result of days upon months of unheralded efforts in the dark of night. The stream of failed attempts is invisible. The long hours spent only to come to a dead end and another new start are not seen by the world – because the world is not watching. It is only when the piece of work is finished that its greatness is realized. To the casual observer, the brilliance seems to have appeared out of nowhere.

It is the same with all great changes. Fundamental shifts do not just happen. They occur over long periods of time. It is just that we cannot see them happening because we do not know what it is that we are seeing.

This is the story of the Quantum Age of IT. The fundamental shifts occurring in the way IT organizations operate appear to be happening at lightning speed and to have come out of nowhere. The changes are coming fast and furiously, but they are not unpredictable. They have been building for years. What we see now is just the final realization of what's been happening in front of our eyes. We just didn't understand what we were seeing.

The seeds were planted in the history of how IT organizations were formed. The structure and culture of the typical IT organization set the stage. But it is three other developments that have occurred during the first years of the new millennium that have put IT organizations on the path to fundamental change. These developments are not new. If you are an IT leader – or even a casual observer of IT, for that matter – these will not be foreign to you. What is new is the realization that, as they combine, they represent a fundamental shift in the relationship between IT and its customers. This shift in relationship has led to the death of IT as we know it and to a fundamentally new IT business model.

To understand this new IT business model and the new paradigm under which the Quantum IT organization will operate, we must first understand how and why the relationship with our customer has changed.

The search box, the social network, and the i that changed the world

There was a day in the not too distant past when you did not have access to the entire world in a matter of moments. For many of us, it is hard to remember such a time. For an entire generation, it is impossible to imagine.

But it has only been during the last decade that Google, Bing and other search technologies have made almost the entire totality of human knowledge available to everyone at a moment's notice. With the advent of mobile technologies, that knowledge has now become truly pervasive – available at almost any time and at any place.

Until that time, the ability to access knowledge was not a trivial matter. Companies spent literally millions upon millions of dollars to capture and harness the unique bits of information that they needed to run their business. Getting access to that data required careful planning and an army of IT people to build, run, and manage the systems that were needed to deliver it. Information and knowledge were critical to the business. But it was not easy to access.

In the year 2000, there were already over 60 million searches performed each day on Google. But by 2011, that same 60 million searches are conducted in under 20 minutes.[4] When Google entered the search game, search was not search as we know it today. At the time, Yahoo! and their various competitors were really online directories – mostly compiled by hand. The phase, 'Google it' had not yet become the phrase that ended every disagreement over some arcane fact. The Internet was still getting its legs and

---

[4] Based upon ComScore data of 4,717,000,000 Google searches per day in 2011.

people were just beginning to understand all of the new possibilities it offered.

Google's stated mission to "organize the world's information and make it universally accessible and useful" changed everything.

Whereas Yahoo! and the other directories at the time served as electronic guidebooks to the new Internet wilderness, Google sought to provide access to knowledge and information. Whatever you were looking for, Google would help you find it. It invested heavily in developing algorithms that helped it decipher the key topics on every page of every website it could find, so that when you searched for that topic, it could deliver what you were looking for.

Most amazingly, it worked. Suddenly, the entire world of knowledge seemed to be only a click away. I remember one of my first experiences with Google was an hour-long session where I just sat and tried to think of the most arcane piece of information I could think to ask and then typed it into that magical, simple search box. Time after time, I came away shocked at how much information was already out there just waiting to be discovered. I think many people had similar experiences. As we did, our trust in the fact that we could find anything grew and grew. Over time, we came to believe that there was essentially no information that we could not get hold of in a matter of minutes.

As this belief in the availability of instant information grew, it caused the first real chasm of trust between IT and its customers. Business executives were not the early adopters of the Internet and search technologies. But as it became more pervasive, they began to be exposed to it. As they did, they were as amazed as the rest of us at the seemingly endless availability of information at their fingertips. They began to discover that they could use this new technology to gain insights into customer expectations and needs and the opinions of their company. They learned that they could use it to gain information about their competitors, government regulations, and global shifts, and countless other pieces of knowledge that was incredibly valuable to them.

But soon this wonder grew to frustration. Why was it that they could get access to all of this information about everything going on around and outside their company, but the information that they needed the most – the information about what was happening *inside* their company – was nearly impossible to get?

A social what?

Search was the first shot across the bow of the 'Battleship IT.' Most IT leaders simply ignored it. They responded to this challenge with a shrug – merely stating that it was not a fair comparison. The kind of internal information that was needed was not something that could be indexed and searched in the same way, they said. The veil of secrecy stayed firmly in place and while the first seeds of doubt and mistrust had been placed, most business executives simply accepted that their internal information was just not going to be as readily accessible as searching for it on Google.

As this process was taking place, however, another new technology was beginning to appear on the horizon that was going to strike a second blow to the relationship between IT and its customers. But if an IT leader were to have seen this second threat emerge, they would have needed to talk to their college-age children.

As has now been chronicled numerous times, Facebook began as a way simply to connect college students to one another, effectively replicating online the dynamic social networks that existed on a college campus. Because of this, Facebook began its life limited to college campuses. You had to have an .edu email address to even open an account. As business or IT leaders, if you heard about it at all, it was as a novelty that your kids were playing with, wasting precious time that would have been better spent studying.

Somewhere along the line, Facebook realized that it was leaving far too much opportunity on the table by limiting its member community to college students, and began opening up its platform to the general public. It exploded. Facebook now has over 800 million members. A huge majority of those members use Facebook on a daily or weekly basis.

While Mark Zuckerberg, the founder of Facebook, created his platform to enable the social interactions of college students, the desire to use his platform to build, nurture, and sustain relationships proved to be universal. The ability to communicate with your social circle through little, offbeat comments; through pictures of yesterday's birthday party; or by sharing a great video you found online proved compelling – to almost everyone. Today, the fastest-growing segment of Facebook users are people over the age of fifty and the vast majority of Facebook users around the world are professionals in the workplace.

While many executives still have a concern with Facebook in the workplace, it has created a subtle, but very real, change in their perception of IT.

It is estimated that approximately 51% of the US population (and 66% of Internet users) now have a Facebook account. Further, a full 92% of Facebook users are of working age.[5] It is not a big leap to assume, then, that well over two-thirds of the employees in a typical US corporation have a Facebook account. You are probably one of them. I know that I am. The vast majority of us, however, do not use Facebook for work, or at work, so what does it matter? It matters because we go home at night and use Facebook to collaborate with our social network. We share information about what we are working on or what we find interesting. We offer and ask for recommendations on everything from new books to the best restaurants to new ways to solve some tricky problem. We post photos and travel logs of our latest vacation. We share videos of our son's sixth birthday party. We plan our upcoming high-school reunion.

In short, we communicate and collaborate.

We do not call it this, of course, because the term 'collaboration' is really just the term we use to describe the natural sharing of information and joint efforts made when we're working to solve a common problem. In our normal lives, it's just what we do. In a corporate setting, rife with bureaucracy and fiefdoms, we need a word to describe the effort to create what should otherwise be effortless.

Our IT customers are no different. They, too, are using Facebook in their personal lives now. They use it to communicate with their college-age children, with their siblings, with their high-school or college friends. They share information, they plan events. And as they have seen

---

[5] Source: SocialBakers.com – United States Facebook Statistics.

the power of this type of dynamic, real-time interaction, they have started to wonder why they cannot have the same kind of experience at work.

One day, it dawns on them.

They have better information about the recent trip to Italy that their second cousin twice removed just took with her family than they do about the next quarter's plans for the business unit whose executive sits down the hall. Why? Why is it that the communication and collaboration that is so easy to achieve in their personal lives is in such short supply in their professional lives. And if this technology exists out there today – and is free – why is it that IT keeps telling them that accessing, sharing, and collaborating with real-time information that actually means something to their business is so hard to do?

"The iPad will never be taken seriously in corporate America"

It was a large room filled with people. It was the middle of 2010 and at the front of the room sat three respected CIOs from well-known companies. In the audience were a wide mix of other CIOs and IT executives from around the country, all there to share in a conversation about the future of the Cloud and other emerging technologies. As the conversation gathered steam, the subject turned to the relatively new iPad and what the CIOs at the front of the room thought about its use in their environments.

"The iPad is a cool piece of technology and there will be a few executives who want to use it, but the iPad will never be taken seriously in corporate America," said one of the CIOs. The others nodded in agreement.

2: Consumerization, Clouds and a Change in Perspective

While Google was changing the perception of the accessibility of information and Facebook was becoming the collaboration platform of the masses, both of them chipping away at the relationship between IT and its customers, one other player was plotting a new device that would eventually become a tipping point in the perception that our customers have of IT.

In 2007, Apple released the first iPhone.

It shook the mobile world and fundamentally changed the relationship people had with their cell phones. Despite the existence of Treos and BlackBerrys at the time, the iPhone truly ushered in the modern era of the smartphone. But while the iPhone was a fundamental shift in many ways, what would eventually become its two most profound elements were initially unnoticed.

The first was the genius of the App Store. The iPhone was, in fact, much more than a phone. The concept of special-function 'apps' that could be loaded to provide any number of functions was a game-changer. It caused a fundamental shift in how people thought of and interacted with their phone. It transformed the iPhone into something altogether different – a multifunctional tool that enabled them to interact with their world in entirely new ways.

What was also not recognized was that, in the iPhone, Apple had created a grand vision for the 'freeing' of information from the confines of clunky computers to truly mobile devices that would be with you at all times. They had created a platform that through the use of innovative design principles and a vast selection of specialized applications would allow people to interact with data and information dynamically and freely. This platform would eventually expand with the release of the first iPad in 2010.

While the pundits were initially skeptical about the usefulness of this new 'tablet' category, it soon became clear that customers loved it. With the iPad, they now had ready access to vast amounts of information, the ability to take notes, the ability to stay connected and to interact – all in a comfortable form more convenient than carrying a laptop around, but more functional than using a smartphone. Most importantly, the design elements and access to the now thousands and thousands of apps provided a simple means to interact with data.

Like the CIOs sitting at the front of that conference room, many people were surprised by the ferocity with which knowledge workers adopted the iPad and began applying it in a business setting. Executives did not wait for IT to 'approve' them. They just bought them, brought them to the office and demanded that they be connected. In many organizations iPads started appearing at meetings in the hands of executives who had never before bothered to carry around a laptop. They had learned that they could load the information they needed for the day and carry it all around on this simple device.

Much like the revelations of the instant availability of information that they discovered through Google and the ease with which they could communicate and collaborate with Facebook, the Apple iPhone and iPad opened customers' eyes to the ease with which they could integrate the dynamic use of information into their everyday lives. And like the others, the rapid adoption of the iPad dealt another blow to the increasingly fragile relationship between IT and its customers.

Business executives and knowledge workers everywhere found themselves asking some fundamental questions.

Through what is now commonly called the 'consumerization of IT,' they were becoming empowered by a vast array of new consumer-driven technologies that had significant business application. These technologies offered entirely new ways to work, new ways to be productive and new ways to think about solving business problems. But none of these new solutions was being offered by their internal IT organizations. In fact, in many cases their internal IT organizations were outright fighting the introduction of these technologies out of fear of security concerns and loss of control. It seemed that there were examples everywhere of technology that was simple to use and just worked. It just didn't exist within their own organizations. Even though they understood that there was more to it, many business executives could not help but be left with a disquieting thought:

"Maybe all of this technology stuff isn't really as complicated as my IT department is trying to make me believe."

The day technology became the business

In the early 1990s, I began a new job at a healthcare company. I was managing technical operations and the first thing I did was visit the major departments that my team and I were supposed to be supporting. As I walked up to the admitting department, I saw a stack of forms sitting next to each of the AS/400 terminals.

"What are those?" I asked the Admitting Manager.

"Downtime forms," she responded nonchalantly.

"Why do you keep them out?"

"Because our systems are constantly going down. There is really no point in putting them away."

I was shocked. At that moment, I was wondering what I had gotten myself into. I clearly had a big job ahead of me. But as disturbing a reflection as that was on the poor service that we were providing at that point, it was also indicative of something else. Technology was not really all that critical to the business.

Yes, it was important and could make things a lot easier. But if those systems failed, the impact was lost productivity and frustration. Business, however, continued. Having our systems fail several times a day was a source of frustration for that Admitting Manager, but in the end she was not that upset because it was not going to really stop her from doing her job.

Today, many people in IT have no idea that there was ever such a thing as a 'downtime form.' Systems are now so critical to the day-to-day operation of almost every business that when systems fail, people go home. Or worse. When computers and complex IT systems began entering the corporate space, they were typically used for back-office functions. Their initial purpose was to automate repetitive and resource-intensive tasks. But generally speaking, these activities happened behind the scenes. If those systems failed, that productivity gain was lost, but business continued as it always had.

As we entered the 'information age,' that began to change. Companies realized that technology could be used to automate and facilitate customer transactions and other elements of the customer relationship. What had been purely a back-office function began to move to the forefront of businesses everywhere. In addition, even in the back office, the application of technology became more entwined into every aspect of business operations. In early incarnations, technology solutions were applied, in isolation, to specific elements of a business process. As companies discovered that they could further increase efficiencies and productivity by automating entire end-to-end business processes, whole business functions became dependent on IT systems to function at all.

It was no longer as simple as having a downtime form to manually complete a process. Now, when systems failed, business came to a stop. And that began to make IT customers very nervous.

When IT was primarily used to automate the back office, business executives and other customers were generally fine with not understanding what was really happening in the basement. They did not want to know what was going on under the covers. They just wanted the value from the increased efficiency and productivity. If things did not always work perfectly, they could live with it.

But as IT became the fuel that drove the entire business, it was a different story. The stakes grew much higher and the impact of failure became exponentially more expensive in all forms. The problem was that the fundamental relationship that existed between IT and its customer had not changed with the shift in application. IT still largely operated as a black box. Put money and requirements in, get a technology solution out. As a business executive whose entire livelihood now depended on technology that you did not understand and could not control, this was a scary position.

The fear caused by this new reality has manifested itself in many ways. In some cases, business executives and managers have crawled inside IT, making it their business to know where every one of their critical applications is running and having the home phone numbers of the people responsible for them. In others, they simply set up their own 'shadow' IT organizations in their own business units so that they could more closely control and watch over these critical functions. In other cases, elaborate IT governance structures have been put in place to try to peel away the veil of secrecy from IT spending and operational decisions.

None of these solutions is ideal. But they are all a reaction to the reality that as the capability of technology and IT systems grew, it became entwined with the very fabric of almost every business organization. The problem is that most IT organizations do not fully realize how vulnerable and helpless this has made many of their customers feel. In almost all organizations, technology has now become a fundamental component of the business. It is no longer this thing that sits off to the side that merely adds some efficiency or productivity. Technology is the business – and that leaves business executives, managers and owners searching for ways to understand and control it much more than they have historically been able to do.

Coupled with the seeds of doubt and mistrust that the consumerization of IT has sown, the now apparent criticality of IT has left business executives and managers searching for options to reduce risk and dependency, and to gain greater control of one of the most critical aspects of their business.

2: Consumerization, Clouds and a Change in Perspective

A new world of competition

Mark Benioff was sure of one thing in 1999: that we were coming to the end of the software technology model and the software business model as we knew it then. He could see the inefficiency of the current approaches to enterprise software and the potential of using the Internet to change the paradigm. After spending over a decade at Oracle and being an early investor in Siebel, he understood the way that enterprise software worked. And he knew where it did not. He saw that customers were ready for something different, something new. The high cost of the licenses themselves, coupled with the cost of support, customization, hardware, training, and staff, made buying and maintaining Customer Relationship Management software in-house a very expensive – and painful – proposition. He knew that there was a better way.

Many things contributed to the success of Salesforce.com. But, undoubtedly, one of the primary factors was that sales and marketing professionals were hungry for a way to seize control of their own destiny. From the beginning, Salesforce.com set its sights squarely on the customer – not on IT and sometimes not even on the sales or marketing executive. The focus was on the person actually using their software. Most of the time, especially at the beginning, IT was not even aware of the discussions until after the deal had been done. Like the iPad and other similar technologies, IT was seen not as an enabler, but often as a barrier to the adoption of this new approach. Salesforce.com and internal executives would often go to great lengths to stay 'off the radar' of the CIO for fear that engaging IT would just slow things down.

Like many others in IT, I watched the entrance of Salesforce.com to the market with interest. But I did not view it as a threat. Sure, there would be those who would try it out, but no major organization would trust this critical function to this type of delivery model. What I, and many others in IT, missed was how frustrated and vulnerable our customers were feeling. While we saw Salesforce.com as unproven and risky, they actually saw the internal IT organization as more risky. The opacity of their internal IT function and the resulting vulnerability that was left in its wake outweighed any risk of this new start-up. Moreover, they were finally dealing with an organization that was solely focused on providing a solution to their most pressing needs – and with a pricing model that was easy to understand. It was a breath of fresh air for business executives. It did take some time for those executives to overcome the historical bias that internal functions were provided by internal IT organizations, but once they did, organizations of all sizes embraced this new approach.

While most did not realize it at the time, Salesforce.com ushered in a new era of competition for the internal IT organization.

Today there are thousands of companies providing directly to business customers services that just a few years ago could only be provided by internal IT organizations. Under the banner of Cloud offerings or 'software-as-a-service,' they provide a wide range of dynamically provisioned services directly to business customers, allowing them to solve specific business problems. While IT people may provide a range of reasons why these providers are not good choices or how they bring with them too much risk, one simple fact remains: they offer business customers the thing that they want the most – choice.

If you believe that this is a passing fad, you are very much mistaken. This is a trend that will only continue to grow and expand. Today there are service providers in every corner of industry, serving even the smallest segments. From broad platforms such as Salesforce.com to niche players such as Locus Technologies that provide on-demand software to manage environmental and energy data, customers have more choice than they ever dreamed of having.

Make no mistake about it. IT is no longer the only game in town. Competition has arrived.

This new competition is really the final piece of the puzzle – the piece that finally changes things for good. Up to this point, IT leaders could shrug off the other concerns and doubts because, frankly, there were no other options. Outsourcing has always been an option and a source of competition, but the costs and effort associated with that were extreme. And, in the end, outsourcing was not really a new business model or approach – just a shift in how internal IT was delivered and paid for.

This new breed of service provider is something altogether different. Like Salesforce.com, these fierce competitors deliver very narrow service offerings designed to solve specific business problems and provide direct, quantifiable business value. These services can be delivered with minimal infrastructure investment and typically offer the ability to provision services on demand. It is nothing like the way most internal IT organizations operate and it creates a sharp contrast between them and their internal IT competitors. And they make sure that the customer knows it.

These organizations offer business executives and managers what they really want – a way to get greater control and transparency over their technology investments. They allow them to remove the fear and sense of vulnerability that they have felt for so many years. This is why most IT leaders are having trouble fighting this new threat. They are attempting to compete on the virtues of security and technology features. But the customer is buying freedom from fear. They are buying an end to feelings of vulnerability. And they are buying control of technology services that are critical to their success.

This commoditization of IT services and the competition it has brought is the third and final element that has fundamentally changed the world in which IT operates.

The way things have always been is not how they will be in the future

Through the consumerization of IT, business leaders and workers of all types had their perceptions changed. They were exposed to technology that worked – simply, seamlessly and inexpensively. It caused them to question what they have been hearing from their internal IT organizations. It began to erode trust as they were confronted on a daily basis with the disparity between their technology at home and their technology at work.

As the criticality of their IT systems increased, IT's customers became increasingly concerned. They felt helpless and vulnerable. Yet IT organizations did not fully understand what was happening, so they simply ignored it. To IT organizations it was business as usual, but their customers were reaching boiling point. There was simply too much at stake to allow things to continue as they were.

With the emergence of third-party providers offering services that had previously only been available from the IT organization, the third and crucial piece of the puzzle fell into place – competition. Now, customers had a real choice. They had a way to overcome their feelings of vulnerability and to begin to harness the power of these new consumer-driven technologies.

As IT professionals, we know that it is not that simple. But frankly, that doesn't matter. This is our customer's reality. They are exercising their right to make the decisions that they feel are best for their business. In many cases, that now means going around and outside IT to get their technology services.

Whether we like it or not, our customers are making a statement: the way things have always been is not how they will be in the future.

If we want their business, things are going to have to change.

Chapter 2 key points

Things just don't change overnight. This is true of the Quantum Age of IT. While it may feel like everything is changing at lightning speed, it has been happening in front of us for well over a decade. But there are three key changes that have occurred in the last several years that have put us on a course to enter the Quantum Age.

Here are the key points you should remember from this chapter:

- Google (along with other search engines) has completely changed our relationship with knowledge. We now expect to be able to get any information that we want or need instantly. And that expectation has now seeped into customer's expectations of what they should get from their IT organizations.

- Facebook has changed the way we all look at both communication and collaboration. We now expect to be able to share information instantly and to collaborate dynamically without barriers.

- Through the iPhone, the iPad, and the rash of other tablets that followed, corporate executives have become accustomed to having all of the information they need at their fingertips, wherever and whenever they need it – and they can't figure out why they can't get this kind of value from their own IT organizations.

- As technology has moved from simply automating back-end functions to being integrated into every aspect of business operations and the customer experience, non-IT executives have become more and more concerned with the state of IT and their dependence on it.

- Finally, the rise of Cloud Computing and software-as-a-service providers has ushered in a new era of competition for IT organizations – we are no longer the only game in town.

- The confluence of these events and changes has led to a simple, yet undeniable conclusion: the way things have always been is not how they will be in the future. IT organizations must change.

PART II

THE NEW IT BUSINESS MODEL: STRATEGIC SOURCER OR STRATEGIC INNOVATOR

CHAPTER 3: WALMART OR NORDSTROM? (WHY YOU MUST CHOOSE WHICH YOU WILL BE)

You wake up on a Saturday morning and you head down to your local Walstrom store.

You have a Walstrom in your neighborhood, right? They are that big retailer who has everything at the lowest price possible. They are the low-cost leader who will beat anyone on price. But they also pride themselves on the greatest, individual service that money can buy.

You've never been there, but it sounds perfect. So you decide to try it out. You walk in and you meet Frank, the store manager.

"Welcome to Walstrom!" he says, enthusiastically. "How can I be of great of service to you?"

You are somewhat taken back by the warehouse kind of feel, but he seems very friendly, so you listen as Frank goes on to extol the virtues of their great store. He explains their mission to be the one-stop shop for all of your retail needs, that everything is provided at the lowest price in the industry and with the greatest service in the industry. He goes on to explain how they provide everyone with 'velvet-glove' treatment and finishes his energized pitch by explaining their 'no-hassle' return policy. He hunches over as if letting you in on a secret and whispers, "Heck, even if you didn't buy something here, we'll take it back!"

You are duly impressed. You think to yourself that you could not possibly ask for more. As it turned out, the reason you came in in the first place was that your Aunt Edna had given you a lovely pair of cashmere shorts that just were not 'your thing,' so you figured this was a good time to try out that return policy.

You explain this to Frank and he says, "Great! Let me direct you to our customer excellence center and they will take great care of you."

With a smile on your face you head back to the 'customer excellence center.' As you turn the corner, the smile disappears. In front of you is a line of about fifty people. Apparently, the customer excellence center was not so excellent.

Undaunted and giving them the benefit of the doubt (everyone has a bad day now and then), you decide that this must be just the place to buy that pair of designer jeans that you had been contemplating. After all, best price and best service is a pretty unbeatable combination. You find the department and begin to look around when one of the 'service associates' approaches and asks if she can help you. You explain that you are looking for a specific brand of jeans.

"Oh, I'm sorry. We actually don't carry that brand," she says with a frown. "In fact, we only carry these three brands of jeans."

"But what about the whole 'most individual service' thing?" you ask. "How can you provide 'individual service' if you only carry three brands of jeans?"

"Sir, in order to keep our prices the lowest possible, we have extremely stringent supply-chain requirements. Only a very few providers can meet them. So I am happy to provide you with excellent service – as long it is with one of these three brands of jeans."

To add insult to injury, she adds, "Have I provided you with excellent service today?"

You leave the store frustrated. While Walstrom offered great promise of being able to deliver it all simultaneously, it had really failed at delivering anything.

The end of the monolithic IT enterprise

Corporate IT is Walstrom.

For almost two generations, the corporate IT organization has tried to do it all. We were the sole-source provider of all technology services to the enterprise. Because of the high costs associated with technology investment, IT has always been under pressure to be a low-cost provider. But that is not how we sold technology investments.

Technology has always been sold as the shiny new gadget. The new way of getting something done better, faster, cheaper. When technology was sold it was never toilet paper. It was always designer jeans. It was always high value to justify the high investment. But with the unstated promise that it was the lowest-cost option available.

So we allowed the paradigm to perpetuate. IT: the monolithic, one-stop, sole-source provider of all things technology, delivering breakthrough advancements that will revolutionize business, all the while at an ever-decreasing cost.

It was unsustainable and we knew it. But we sold it this way because we figured that it was the only way they would buy it. But just like Walstrom, it is a doomed business model. While everyone wants everything for nothing, it is virtually impossible to deliver it successfully.

In promising something that is not possible to deliver, we have ensured a shared frustration with our customers. And they will no longer accept it.

Despite how it may seem at times, our customers do not want empty promises. They want truth, transparency, and options. The consumerization, criticality and commoditization of IT has opened their eyes to their vulnerabilities and, most importantly, to their newfound options.

And they are sending a clear message to corporate IT organizations: *You are no longer the only game in town – so stop acting like you are.*

The 'T' in the road

IT as we know it is dead. The road that we have been on for the past 45 years is coming to an end. Thankfully, it is not a dead end, but we can no longer continue on the same road. We have reached a T, and, as we reach that T in the road, we must make a choice. We must make a right or a left. There is no other option. There is no road forward in the direction in which we have been going. There is only right or left. A choice must be made.

The road that we have been on has been that of the monolithic provider of all IT services. It is no longer practical or profitable for IT to try to maintain the internal capabilities to provide for all of the enterprise's technology needs. The diversity of needs is simply too vast. As our customers have realized the potential for technology to drive business value in new ways, their demands have increased. With every new opportunity to leverage technology for some business need, the complexity of the resulting IT environment increases exponentially. With the consumerization of IT, customer expectations in terms of speed, reliability, and ease of use continue to grow at the same time. It is simply not sustainable.

IT managers know this. You feel as if you are under constant attack. It feels as though you can never make the customer happy. It seems you can never deliver enough to meet their insatiable demand for new, more advanced and more integrated technologies. And yet, they seem blissfully ignorant of the complexity that this brings – of how hard it is to manage such an environment.

So we build walls. We create policies. We establish standards. We try to bring order to the chaos by putting limits on what our customers can do. But all this does is push our customers to our competitors. However well intentioned, these barriers and limits only serve to alienate us from our customers. They reinforce their feelings of vulnerability and lack of control and they make the new options that they are discovering seem that much more enticing.

It is clear that the current IT business model has run its course. A new IT business model is needed that will enable IT organizations to compete in this new era. The new IT business model is not monolithic. It is targeted. It does not try to be the sole provider of IT services. Instead, it seeks to understand how value is derived from the technology investments and to reorient its delivery model appropriately. The choice at the top of the T is a choice between one of two new business models: The Strategic Sourcer or the Strategic Innovator.

3: Walmart or Nordstrom?

One market, two business models

In theory, Walmart and Nordstrom are competitors. In theory.

They are both large retailers. They both provide a wide range of clothing, accessories, and sundry other items to their customers. But that is where the comparison stops. They serve vastly different markets. And they offer significantly different value propositions to those markets.

Walmart is all about delivering essential items at the lowest price possible. Nordstrom is about luxury and service. While, theoretically, they are in the same business, how they must operate to deliver on their promise to their customers is vastly different. For Walmart, it is all about the supply chain and operational efficiency. For Nordstrom, it is all about high quality and the customer experience.

Neither is right or wrong. They are simply serving different customers who perceive value differently. In some cases, the same customer may shop at both Walmart and Nordstrom. But when they do, their value equation adjusts. They do not expect Nordstrom-like service at Walmart, nor do they shop at Nordstrom because they believe they will get the lowest-priced jeans available. They are simply different.

Because they are different, because they serve different markets with different value propositions, they require different business models. As they are both retailers, they will have some things in common, but the fundamentals of how they operate will be very different.

They will not hire employees of the same type. They will not provide the same levels of training. They will not have the same policies in place. They will invest in their enabling technologies differently.

For Walmart, it is all about supply chain. Everything they do is about moving product through the process as quickly and as efficiently as possible. Everything from their systems to their training practices to their return policies is based on this simple fundamental driver. For Nordstrom, it is the customer experience. They, too, have supply-chain systems; they, too, train their people; they, too, have return policies. But they are all very different. They are aligned to their primary driver of ensuring that their customers receive the best service possible.

This makes sense. No one would suggest that Walmart should adopt Nordstrom's return policies and expect them to keep their prices the lowest in the industry. Likewise, no one would suggest that Nordstrom hire low-wage workers, offer them no customer service training, and expect them to maintain the customer experience. They have tuned their systems, processes, practices, and policies to match their business model.

Yet in the world of IT this does not happen.

Regardless of how the company perceives the value of IT, almost all IT organizations look the same and function the same way. The problem is that our customers do not value things equally. Some enterprises are looking for the Walmart value proposition from their IT investments. For them, it is about getting the essential items at the lowest price possible. Other customers are looking for the Nordstrom value proposition. They are looking for truly strategic innovation. They understand that it may cost more, but it is what they need.

3: Walmart or Nordstrom?

Just as Walmart and Nordstrom have developed different business models to deliver against their value promise to their respective markets, so must IT organizations reorient their systems, processes, practices, and policies toward one of the new IT business models and become either a Strategic Sourcer (*à la* Walmart) or a Strategic Innovator (*à la* Nordstrom).

The Strategic Sourcer

I remember walking around a lake in Ohio advising my client. He was a senior IT executive on the rise at a Fortune 500 company and I was telling him that he had no choice – he had to figure out how to create strategic innovation if he wanted to remain relevant. It was 2006 and, the way I saw it, IT was on the verge of being fully commoditized once and for all. My advice to him was that he had to make his customers take notice. He needed to help them realize that the path to competitive differentiation was through the wondrous innovations that IT could bring to the table. He needed to innovate or die. There was no other way to be strategic.

It was great advice, delivered strongly and authoritatively.

And it was dead wrong.

His company was a large manufacturer. They sold a physical product in many different forms, but it all essentially came down to a few core components – and none of them were driven by technology or information. Was IT important to their organization? Of course. But it was important in that in enabled them to drive efficiency into their production life cycle and it allowed them to automate otherwise laborious tasks. But were they ever going to derive truly strategic value at a customer level from their IT investments? Probably not.

They did not need designer jeans. They needed the raw essentials delivered consistently and as inexpensively as possible. They needed Walmart.

The problem was that I was looking at it from my perspective, as an IT professional. Let's face it, toilet paper is not that sexy. I wanted IT to be cool. I wanted this IT executive to deliver the pizzazz. Blinded by the desire that I wanted IT to be innovative, I failed to see how the customer was really going to harness value from their IT investments. I was not looking at things from the customer's perspective. I was looking at it from mine.

I remember discussing this with someone after the fact and they asked, "But if IT is just about delivering the bare essentials at the cheapest price, doesn't that just reduce IT to a commodity and guarantee that we will all get outsourced?"

It was an interesting question, but it missed the point. Was the technology a commodity? Perhaps. But did that mean that the IT organization that provided it was commoditized? Not necessarily. This is where I missed it while walking around that lake. I was confusing what made a strategic technology with what made a strategic organization. You do not need the technology to be strategic for the IT organization to be a strategic asset to the enterprise. Being strategic is about enabling the strategy of the enterprise. By doing so, you create value. If the strategy of the organization is to reduce costs and improve efficiency so that the organization can compete in a highly competitive and price-sensitive industry, then any technology investments that either reduce the cost platform of the technology itself or deliver that type of efficiency and cost reduction to other parts of the organization are strategic.

That is what being a 'Strategic Sourcer' means. It recognizes that in the value model of the customer, technology in most cases is not going to drive value through technology-enabled innovation. In this model, strategic value is derived from developing and managing highly efficient supply chains that deliver the technology services that the organization needs, as inexpensively as possible. Technology is needed to run the business. That does not change. But because that technology is almost exclusively overhead, the job of the Strategic Sourcer is to develop highly dynamic models to deliver those needed services with as little waste and friction as possible. Little value is delivered by building these technology services 'in-house' because there is little intrinsic value to be gained by doing so.

This can be tough for IT leaders to accept because we like to see ourselves as purveyors of the future. But it is this perception that inhibits our ability to become true partners to our customer. The fact of the matter is that they are buying toilet paper. It may not be sexy, but it is essential.

This is why it is so critical that you begin by understanding your core business model. If you find that your enterprise's value model is that they need the Walmart of IT, then you must accept it, embrace it and begin building your delivery capabilities against it. But there is one more thing. It is critical that you take to heart one vital fact: being a Strategic Sourcer is very, very strategic.

This is what I failed to grasp while walking around that lake. Strategic value comes in many forms. Realizing that you are needed to be a Strategic Sourcer is not a sign of failure or a sign that something is missing. It is simply a recognition of how and your customers value their IT investments. If you think that this somehow makes you less valuable to the organization, you will be very wrong. In some ways, you become even more valuable. In industries where success is defined by fractions of a point in margin or milliseconds in faster delivery time, the smallest contributions to efficiency and cost performance are vital. There is very little margin of error in organizations of these types. In many cases, the only competitive advantage that they will find will be in the additional efficiency or cost reduction that they can get from their IT investments.

Look at it this way. In the comparison between Walmart and Nordstrom, which of their supply-chain management systems is more critical to their business success? It is important for Nordstrom, but their value is derived from the customer experience. But at Walmart, their value is derived from their ability to save a percentage or two in costs from each product. If their supply chain is less than the best in the industry, they will fail in their mission.

Being a Strategic Sourcer is an extremely valuable business model and one that has the potential to drive significant value to the enterprise. It requires that you orient your policies, processes, governance structures, and practices around a simple mission: acquiring and delivering technology services to your customers as efficiently and as inexpensively as possible. It may not be glamorous, but, for the customers of a Strategic Sourcer, it is vital.

The Strategic Innovator

In 1978, Fred Smith had a revelation. The CEO of FedEx realized that when someone needed to get a package someplace quickly, the delivery of the package was only half of the equation. He realized that his customers needed to get a package delivered quickly, but that, beyond rapid delivery, they were also buying a sense of security. They wanted a way to be sure that their precious delivery had made it where they needed it to arrive – on time. "The information about the package is just as important as the package itself," he said.

Working together, Fred Smith and his CIO, Jim Barksdale, perfected a comprehensive set of tools that would enable them to track their packages at a very high level of detail from the moment of pickup to the moment of delivery[6] – and, most importantly, share that information with their customers. Almost all of the technology had to be built from the ground up. Nothing like it existed in the marketplace. It was big and complex, requiring full integration into the fundamental business processes of the organization. But it was all worth it.

When FedEx (then known as Federal Express) released their first version of their online package tracking tools, it completely changed the game. People were immediately smitten with the ability to track their precious cargo every step of the way. They were no longer relegated to hoping that their package had made it, anxiously waiting for phone confirmation from the recipients. Now, they were in control. When we first experienced this new technology,

---

[6] The development of the COSMOS Package Tracking System was started under the leadership of Charlie Brandon.

most of us sat there refreshing the page multiple times over the course of a day – just enjoying the ability to watch our package move throughout the country. It gave us a sense of empowerment. It made us feel secure and comfortable that our package was in good hands. And it made FedEx the dominant carrier of overnight deliveries in the industry for more than three decades.

This is the role of the Strategic Innovator.

In some industries and for some businesses, technology has the power to create competitive advantage through the application of technology to improve or enhance the customer experience. This is most prominent in industries in which information and technology are key components of the product or service being delivered. In those cases, executives are looking for their IT organizations to help them leverage technology to break through competitive barriers and create advantage.

It is important to recognize here that this is not about technology innovation. A Strategic Innovator is focused on creating technology-enabled business innovation. When FedEx introduced their package tracking system, it was not that they had developed some amazing new technology from scratch. What they had done was create a novel way to apply technology to create business innovation – to improve the customer experience and to deliver greater value to their customer. Strategic innovation is focused solely on the enterprise's customers. Innovating a new way to manage the network infrastructure or a better way to architect your application platforms may provide much value in terms of operations or costs, but that is not what strategic innovation is all about.

The Strategic Innovator business model is one which is structured and organized with almost the sole purpose of creating customer value through the unique application of technology. Operations are not their core competency or chief concern. Their value comes not from efficiency and cost savings as much as from creating unique value for the customer that results in competitive advantage. There are many examples of this type of strategic innovation – and they are almost always associated with market leaders and progressive companies. Consider the value created from these strategic innovations:

- Amazon's Recommendation System: This system changed the online purchasing experience and resulted in a much more personal interaction than most felt was possible when it was released. Their recommendation engine now accounts for 30% of its sales.[7]

- Progressive Insurance's Price Comparison System: This unique application of technology enables potential customers to instantaneously compare Progressive's prices with those of its competitors. This innovation, along with a long string of others, has helped propel Progressive from $1.2 billion in premiums written in 1990 to $13 billion in 2004.[8]

- Chase Bank's iPhone Check Deposit System:[9] This innovation applied technology that for the most part already existed within the bank and simply created

---

[7] Source: "Building with Big Data," *The Economist*, May 26, 2011.
[8] Source: Richard L. Daft, *Organization Theory and Design* (2006).
[9] USAA was the first commercial bank to offer Remote Deposit Capture (RDC) in 2009. However, it was Chase's adoption, inclusion in an iPhone application, and subsequent promotion that introduced it to the market more generally.

an interface that enabled customers to deposit checks using their iPhone. It is resulting in benefits across the board: increases in new customer satisfaction, improved customer loyalty and reduced transaction costs.

These types of innovation have a direct impact on the customer experience and value perception. Because of this, they cannot be created in a vacuum or by IT alone. Neither can they be created by the business unit alone. This type of innovation can only be created through tight integration between IT and its customers. It is why an IT organization that is a Strategic Innovator must look hard at its structure, its processes, and its governance models. Everything needs to be restructured to create the tight integration of IT into fundamental business planning and operational models.

The driving force at FedEx has never been IT. IT was critical and created strategic, competitive advantage for the organization, but it was always an enabler. The driving force behind every innovation at FedEx was deeply rooted in two primary objectives: (a) fulfill the promise to the customer and (b) execute flawlessly in order to fulfill that promise. Those core objectives were not IT objectives; they were business objectives. By focusing on these two elements, the FedEx team was able to create game-changing innovations, while simultaneously reducing costs. By working together to develop the tools that would become the foundation of FedEx's relationship with its customers, the executive team did not operate as if they each had their own separate job in the process. Instead, they saw themselves as having the same job – enhancing customer experience and providing the sense of security that their customers desired – but they brought to their shared job different perspectives.

This level of engagement, this change in the perception of the roles that both IT and the customer play, must occur at all levels of the organization. This is not something that can only happen at the top. Bill Wray realized that he needed to create just this type of atmosphere when he took over as CIO of Blue Cross Blue Shield of Rhode Island. He saw that his team had become too insular and not focused enough on how their technology impacted patients and the delivery of care. So he put his people in the field. At all levels of the organization, his goal was to "get the people doing the work in touch with the people that need the work." Because the business model of the Strategic Innovator is driven predominately by the enterprise's customer, it demands a different set of skills and a different type of relationship at all levels of the IT organization. Most of all, it requires that the IT organization become, as Bill Wray says it, "much more forward-deployed."

While playing the role of Strategic Innovator can be exciting and enticing, it is not without its risks and drawbacks. It takes a certain amount of leadership courage to commit the IT organization to creating this kind of innovation. As a Strategic Innovator, running a tight shop is not enough. You will be expected to deliver such game-changing breakthroughs on a consistent basis. You will also need to balance the need to build an organization that has the freedom to explore, to be creative, and to innovate, against simultaneously managing – at least at some level – ongoing operations. Managing those different skill sets will be a challenge. But while there are risks and challenges with the Strategic Innovator business model, the payoff is huge. As a Strategic Innovator, IT is able to impact the lives of customers directly and meaningfully. It has its risks and challenges, but to the Strategic Innovator's customers, IT will be one of the best investment decisions they ever make.

'Choosing' your new IT business model

So, which will it be?

Are you going to lead your IT organization through a transformation leading to it becoming a Strategic Sourcer or a Strategic Innovator?

Unfortunately, it's not that simple. Or – more to the point – it is actually not your choice.

The choice between being a 'Strategic Innovator' and a 'Strategic Sourcer' is really about understanding what your customer values. Are they looking for a Walmart or a Nordstrom experience? Before you answer, the truth is that you probably don't know. There are two reasons for this.

First, you've probably never asked them. This is just not something that we typically talk about in IT organizations. In the state of constant growth, there's not been the time. But this is not a choice as much as it is an agreement. The first step to making this 'choice' is to come to an explicit understanding with your customer regarding what they value from their IT investments. But before you run off to have this conversation with your customer, you need to tackle the second reason why you probably don't have a good answer: your customer probably doesn't know what they value or why.

Let's face it, for the last 45 years your customer has been shopping at Walstrom. Until the recent advent of Cloud providers, it was all that they knew. And just like you, they've been too busy to enjoy the luxury of contemplating their wish list. They simply worked with the IT organization that they had and got the best that they could from the process.

It is also not as simple as it might seem at first blush to understand how and why a customer might value their IT investments differently. I was working with a senior director in a large financial institution and discussing the relative criticality of their various systems on business operations. I had largely considered them to be a Strategic Innovator, but as we began talking through the different systems and how they supported or contributed to the various business processes, it became clear that, in their case, their business value and competitive advantage had very little to do with their technology. They really should be operating more like a Strategic Sourcer.

The decision of whether the Strategic Sourcer or Strategic Innovator business model is best for your enterprise is one that will require that you have a series of long and intense conversations with your business customers. They must understand that the current model is not sustainable or beneficial for either of you. You must help them understand the benefits and trade-offs of each business model and then have a frank and honest conversation with them about what is most appropriate to the enterprise. This can be a challenging process. There are organizations, like that financial institution, that are operating much more like Strategic Innovators, with their high cost structures and heavy business-unit integration, when they really should be operating like Strategic Sourcers. And there are organizations who are treating their IT organizations as Strategic Sourcers, looking for them to drive every ounce of efficiency and cost savings out of the organization, when they should be operating as Strategic Innovators and as a result are missing valuable opportunities to realize strategic value from their investments.

There is a choice to be made, but you must make this decision with your customer. Your mutual success depends on it. Once you have chosen, you will have a solid benchmark against which to structure and develop your organization. You should consider everything to be on the table. Your organizational structure, your processes, your policies, your hiring practices, your training standards – everything should be reevaluated based on your new business model.

It will be the first real step toward becoming a Quantum Age IT organization.

Laying the groundwork for your new IT business model

Making the decision as to whether you will be Walmart or Nordstrom sounds simple. But the ramifications of that decision are significant. They will require that you fundamentally look at all aspects of how you operate and organize the IT function. As IT organizations begin aligning to one of these two business models, stark differences will emerge. But there will also be a strong, common foundation that all Quantum IT organizations will be built upon.

Just as Walmart and Nordstrom are both in the retail sector, and, therefore, both have highly developed supply chains, so too must all Quantum IT organizations begin to focus extensively on developing and managing their supply chains and value networks.

In that truth lies perhaps the greatest change that the Quantum Age represents: IT organizations must shift their fundamental operating model from being primarily a manufacturer to being a retailer.

Up to this point in our history, there has been little choice. IT organizations had to build most of the services that they delivered. As our industry has matured, that has changed. There are independent providers of core applications and infrastructure services available in almost every industry sector today. The primary role of the IT organization must, therefore, shift away from primarily building to primarily sourcing and managing – regardless of whether you are a Strategic Sourcer or a Strategic Innovator.

Despite their wildly different value propositions and corresponding business models, neither Walmart nor Nordstrom invests much of their capital or human resources in manufacturing. When there is value-driven need, they may contract to have something manufactured exclusively for their customers, but they recognize that the value they provide is derived from a retail transaction, not from manufacturing. The same will be true for Quantum IT organizations.

As such, the core competencies must shift. Much greater value must be placed on the skills required to develop and manage highly intricate networks of suppliers to deliver the value that your customers need. It is the foundation upon which the Quantum Age IT organization will be built.

Chapter 3 key points

Corporate IT organizations have tried to do it all. We have tried to simultaneously be the 'low-cost leader' and the 'strategic partner.' And for the most part it hasn't worked out to well. With the increase in competition, organizations need to become highly attuned to the needs of their business customers and make a choice. Will you be a 'Strategic Sourcer' or a 'Strategic Innovator'?

Here are the key points you should remember from this chapter:

- While Walmart and Nordstrom are theoretically in the same market, they serve vastly different markets. Therefore, they have vastly different hiring and training practices and different policies, and invest in technology differently.

- IT organizations need to stop acting as if every organization is the same and begin aligning the entire operating model to whether they must become a Strategic Sourcer or Strategic Innovator.

- Being a Strategic Sourcer is very strategic. While the technology may be commoditized, it will be how it is applied in concert with the business objectives that will make the IT function strategic.

- The role of the Strategic Innovator is to create competitive advantage through the application of technology to improve or enhance the customer experience.

- But it's not about being a technology innovator as much as it's about creating technology-enabled business innovation.

- You must choose your IT business model based on how your customer values its investments in IT – it's not your choice.

- This leads to perhaps the greatest paradigm shift that is occurring in IT – we are moving from being manufacturers of technology to becoming retailers of technology – this means that the fundamental approaches that we take to how we organize ourselves and the skills we develop must change.

CHAPTER 4: MASTERING THE SUPPLY CHAIN AND THE VALUE NETWORK

You never know what life may throw at you. Sometimes, just when you think you've finally figured it out, the situation just changes. It's at that point that you have a choice to make.

The first 35 years of Ray Kroc's life were not the stuff of business legend. He quit high school without graduating to enlist during World War I. At the end of the war he became a jazz pianist, then a salesman for the Lily-Tulip Cup Company, then a musical director for a Chicago radio station, then he sold Florida real estate, then back to Lily-Tulip, eventually rising to the position of a regional sales manager.

Then in 1937, his ship came in.

He came across the Prince Castle Multi-Mixer, which was able to make five milk shakes at one time. By the early 1940s he had formed a company and became the exclusive distributor of the product. In the post-World War II era, business boomed. Ray Kroc had finally settled down and things had started to become a bit more comfortable. But it wouldn't stay that way.

By the early 1950s, sales were plummeting as the market shifted. He could see that things were changing and so he opened his eyes to new opportunities. That openness brought him to San Bernardino, California in 1954 to visit a restaurant owned by Mac and Dick McDonald. They had recently purchased eight of his Multi-Mixers and he wanted to see what was different about their business.

The rest, as they say, is history. Ray Kroc immediately saw the potential of the McDonald brothers' new business model and entered into an agreement with them to take over the expansion of their franchise operation. McDonalds as we now know it was born.

Ray Kroc had a choice in the face of his plummeting sales. He could resist and continue to fight the shifts in the market or he could realize that the market was shifting in ways that he could not control and instead adapt to it. It is likely that this was not something that he wanted. After years of failure and uncertainty, things had finally been good. But his years of struggle had taught him that things always change and he was, therefore, willing to adapt. However, this adaption was more than just a minor detour. It represented a fundamental shift in business model.

IT leaders find themselves standing in same place that Ray Kroc found himself in. After years of struggle and work, many IT organizations have finally begun to find some sense of stability. IT is a part of the fabric of almost every organization. But just as it happened to Ray Kroc, the market is shifting beneath your feet. The choices are the same – stand and resist or accept that you cannot control the market and adapt.

Adapting to become a Quantum IT organization will not be easy. It will require a fundamental shift in almost all aspects of how you think of your business, your role and your function. But there is simply no alternative.

The question is, however, what will it mean to transition from being a manufacturer to being a retailer?

From manufacturing to retail

When we think about it for a moment, we realize that the shift from being primarily a manufacturer to being a retailer has been happening for some time. It actually explains many of the challenges that IT organizations have had relating to their customers. That is because what has been happening is that while you have continued to think of yourself and operate as a manufacturer, your customers have begun to see you as a retailer – with all of the expectations that come with that perception. The latest buzz about the 'consumerization of IT' is simply the latest manifestation of a reality that has been evolving for a long time.

In this realization, we can find the source of many of the challenges and disconnects in our customer relationships:

- Manufacturers are focused on engineering, design, and efficiency of production. Retailers are concerned with the customer experience, product selection, and merchandising (the positioning, packaging, and promotion of their wares).

- Manufacturers increase earnings by engineering products to their deemed quality standards (to reduce defects, waste, and returns) and by increasing production efficiency. Retailers increase earnings primarily by introducing exciting new products, increasing customer loyalty, and identifying and promoting high-margin products.

- Manufacturers operate in a capital-intensive space and are most concerned with the systems of production. Retailers operate in a highly dynamic and fluid space and are most concerned with the transaction.

When you see yourself as a manufacturer, but your customer sees you as a retailer, there develops a fundamental perception divide that cannot be crossed by mere discussion. You and your customer are operating from fundamentally different paradigms, which is why it so often happens that you can leave a meeting in complete agreement – but having agreed to completely different things!

Welcome to the world of retail

The market has shifted. Like it or not, your future is that of a retailer. The good news is that in making this transition you will automatically relieve much of the stress that this disconnect in perception has caused. But it does mean that you need to build some new core capabilities to be effective in your new role.

Whether you need to become a Strategic Sourcer or a Strategic Innovator, this much is certain: the vast majority of your technology and application infrastructure will not live within the walls of your data center. You will only manufacture those parts of your solutions that provide discrete and direct value to your customers and that cannot be purchased or contracted elsewhere. That is the world of retail.

And in this new world, the rules and the capabilities needed to function effectively are different. To compete and thrive in this market, therefore, you need to develop the capabilities that will enable you to function within the retail paradigm:

4: Mastering the Supply Chain and the Value Network

Supply-chain management

The balance of this chapter will discuss the creation and management of both the 'value network' and the 'supply chain' in more depth, but at this point it is important that you hear one key point – managing your supply chain will be far more complex than you anticipate. Manufacturers have supply chains. But they are trafficking in raw materials and the relative complexity is much less than the supply chain required of a major retailer. Today, the vast majority of your supply chain is internally controlled. Its management may get entwined in internal politics, but in the end almost everything you need to deliver your services is under the control of the senior IT executive. As you move into the Quantum Age and become a retailer, that will all change. The vast majority of your supply chain will be outside your control and you will need to be able to manage and coordinate an intricate and highly complex network of suppliers in order to deliver your services to your customers. It will offer distinct advantages, but it will require a skill set completely different from what you have today.

Product management and merchandising

As IT organizations make the transition from manufacturer to retailer, it will require that a discipline be developed to package and promote the services that are 'in production' and available for consumption. You will also need to identify 'market trends' to determine what services will be in demand next. Just as in the retail industry, much of this potential future demand will be driven by external forces. In the retail business, there is a lot of competition. Combating that competition will require significant focus on communications, messaging, and anticipating future needs. IT leaders will need to build capabilities to manage this end-to-end process in order to ensure that rapidly changing customer demands can be anticipated and met.

Customer experience management

While they are wildly different, both Walmart and Nordstrom have a clearly defined and distinct customer experience that they seek to create. They understand who their customer is and the type of experience that they expect, and they build processes and structures to create that experience. IT organizations will need to make the same commitment to developing this capability. This is not as simple as making a commitment to a generic sense of 'good customer service.' IT leaders will need to explicitly define the experience that they intend to deliver to their customers and develop the internal capacity to deliver, measure and manage that experience to create the customer satisfaction and loyalty that they will need to compete.

These are capabilities that are largely absent from the world of the IT manufacturer today. But whether you are a Strategic Sourcer or a Strategic Innovator, they will be the foundation upon which you build your business.

The broker fallacy: aligning your supply chain to your business model

Before we go any further, we need to pause to dispel a fallacy that has managed to get some traction in the industry. Namely, that the future of IT is that it will be merely a broker of technology services. While the transition from manufacturer to retailer means that IT will now be much more focused on managing its supply chain, being in the retail business is not synonymous with being a broker.

A broker provides no value-added context to a transaction except for one – the facilitation of a connection between a supplier and someone in need of whatever the supplier supplies. Nothing more. It is a business model built on scarcity and the control of information. Unless there are other barriers, brokers are useful only when someone is unfamiliar with a market environment. Once you understand how the system works, your first inclination is to 'skip the middleman' and go direct to the supplier. This is why brokers will go to great lengths to protect crucial information and promote the scarcity of supply.

Retail, on the other hand, is a business model that is normally built on a foundation of abundance. Retailers provide the aggregation that a broker might, but they provide a significant amount of value during the transaction. Through the abundance model, retailers provide their customers with a simple way to review the options available and select the best fit. Imagine purchasing all of your clothes through a broker. If you can tell them exactly what brand, color, and size you need, they may be able to optimize the purchasing process for you. But, in most cases, you need the experience of being able to see the options, try things on and compare to make the best decision. Throw in the ability to handle returns when things go wrong, the overall experience that is created, and you can see that there is a tremendous amount of value created during a retail transaction that simply does not exist in a brokerage model.

IT customers are not looking for a broker. They do not want someone whom they have to be able to tell exactly what they need so that that person can go and find it for them. They are looking for someone who will understand the value they seek and build a business model that delivers it. They want you to develop a value network and supply chain that is purpose-built to deliver the value that they need from their technology investments. They want nothing more than to walk into their own customized version of Walmart or Nordstrom and see that everything from the way the aisles are arranged, to the types of product that are carried, to the way that checkout is handled has been built with them in mind.

So, with the broker fallacy put to rest, the question becomes: how do you create this supply chain?

Defining your value network

'Value' may be the most misused and misunderstood word in the world of IT.

How is value created? What does 'value' mean?

These questions are foundational as you lead your organization into the Quantum Age. Fundamentally, value is at the heart of every transaction. For a relationship to be positive and productive, there must be a fair exchange of value. When there is not, the relationship will be strained. We must, therefore, be aware of the value we are providing, when and where that value is being created, and how it is being delivered.

We may not talk in terms of value often, but our perception of value is what influences our decisions and whether we view the transaction in a positive or negative light. For instance, if you buy a bottle of water for $1.50, you are making an implicit statement that the satisfaction you received from that bottle of water was worth the price you paid for it. At a football game, that same bottle of water may cost $4.00. You may grumble about it, but buying it you are implicitly saying that it provides the necessary value to justify the price. Or you may decide that the price is too high and simply walk away. Either way, your perception of value dictates how you view the transaction.

Why does this matter? Because the first step to building a robust and effective supply chain is to define a value network that will create the value your customers expect as your service passes through the supply chain. When an IT organization begins building a supply chain without first seeing it through the lens of a value network, it is doomed to failure. Without understanding how value is created and delivered, it will be like creating an assembly-line manufacturing system without having any idea what you are building.

The concept of a value chain was first introduced by Michael Porter in his seminal book entitled *Competitive Advantage*. The concept was later expanded into the idea of value networks by Clayton Christensen and others. The concept of a value chain was simple: every product or service was the result of a long chain of suppliers, each of which took some output from another and added value to it in some way before passing it up the value chain until it finally reached the ultimate customer. It was only upon reaching the ultimate customer that the sum of the value added at each stage of the chain was extracted and realized. In articulating the concept of a value network, Christensen and others expanded this thinking by recognizing that value was often not created in a simple, linear fashion, but that in modern business, value was created by a network of dynamic and interrelated components that came together to create value for the customer.

While IT organizations do not often think of it in these terms, virtually every service that an IT organization delivers is the result of this kind of highly complex, highly dynamic value network. Defined as a value network, we see that virtually everything that IT does is highly intertwined. The silos that we have created are just that – creations. They do not reflect the reality of how services are constructed and delivered. Instead, these silos represent management attempts to organize the function and cope with the increasing levels of technical expertise and specialization required to operate a modern IT organization. But while those are valid concerns, allowed to evolve unfettered they have come to hinder IT's ability to effectively move a service through the value network so that its value can be fully realized by the customer. Worse, the loss of the value network perspective and the pervasiveness of the silo mentality has allowed IT organizations to forget why they exist in the first place.

To compete in the Quantum Age, this must be corrected. The value network must be restored. You must map every service from the customer's perspective, identifying where and how value is added and applied through the process. You will find that your value network extends far beyond the walls of your data center and organization. Your network of external suppliers will figure significantly into this equation. Once you have mapped out your value network, you will be ready to establish and manage your supply chain.

Creating and managing your supply chain

Whereas a value network is a logical representation of how value is created and multiplied until it is ultimately delivered to your customer, a supply chain is the practical manifestation of that value network. It is not enough to merely *understand* how value is created. Once that understanding exists, it is imperative that its creation be protected at every stage of the process.

Value is fragile. In many cases, value is created only by a tiny margin. Any inefficiency or loss of focus can destroy that value en route.

To most organizations, supply-chain management in the context of the IT function either does not exist or exists only in the form of a Vendor Management Office (VMO) or similar function. Ironically, because value is not typically the focus of the VMO or of vendor management policies, the very efforts to 'control and optimize' vendor relationships often destroy value because they are not designed to manage and protect it. The challenge is that most VMOs are established with an adversarial posture. They see their vendors as organizations that must be beaten down to get the best price and then controlled to meet delivery commitments. If you are strictly in a commodity business, this may be appropriate (Walmart is legendary for the process they put their suppliers through), but for most IT organizations this is an incomplete view.

The challenge is that you cannot know if it is appropriate without understanding how value is created and delivered (which is why you must begin with defining your value network). Once you understand how value is created and delivered, you have a model for establishing and managing your supply chain to protect and enhance that value as it moves through the supply chain. For most IT organizations, that means taking a completely different view of how vendors are selected and managed.

Creating a supply-chain management capability will be a requirement of the Quantum IT organization. Before we explore how to do this in practical terms, it is helpful to understand the concepts of Systems Thinking introduced by Peter Senge in his book *The Fifth Discipline*. In this landmark work, Senge introduces Systems Thinking as the 'fifth discipline' in a suite of disciplines required to create a 'learning organization.' The concepts of Systems Thinking are relevant to building the capability of managing a supply chain because they force a recognition that a supply chain and a value network are not simply collections of independent transactions. Instead, they are a system that operates through a series of interrelated dependencies.

In the book, Senge describes a simulation called the Beer Game. It was originally developed at the MIT Sloan School of Management in the 1960s and is used to demonstrate how a situation is often misinterpreted when someone believes that they are acting independently and fails to recognize that they are in fact acting as part of a highly integrated system. In the simulation, a liquor store stocks a certain brand of beer which consistently sells four cases each week. Through a chance circumstance, demand doubles and sends ripples through the supply chain. The simulation utilizes a simplified three-layer supply chain: the retailer, the distributor, and the manufacturer.

As the simulation plays out, each participant attempts to react, only seeing the situation from their perspective. They do not see the series of transactions as a system, nor do they attempt to manage supply at a systemic level. Each player simply reacts to their individual situation as best they can. The results are dramatic. As Senge describes, the simulation almost always results in a severe shortage followed by a severe oversupply, leading to devastating financial results for all players.

During the simulation recap, most players believe that there was a huge surge in demand that spiked and then abruptly fell off, resulting in the calamity – thus absolving themselves from any responsibility. In fact, however, the simulation makes a single change to the system: doubling demand during week one and sustaining the newly increased demand for the remainder of the simulation.

The lesson of the simulation and the lesson for IT organizations looking to build a supply-chain management capability is that you cannot manage a system by discretely managing its parts. You must instead manage the supply chain holistically at a systemic level. While we may not think of IT services as the 'beer' in the simulation, the same forces are at play as we manage the delivery of services that rely on a complex and intricate network of internal and external service components.

The intersection of systems thinking with the concepts of a value network provide the paradigm that must be applied to effectively manage a complex IT supply chain. By focusing on understanding how value is created through the supply chain and establishing a structure to systemically manage the supply chain to protect that value, you will be able to consistently deliver services effectively and efficiently.

Building your supply-chain management capability

Understanding that a 'value network' and 'Systems Thinking' are the keys to effectively managing the IT supply chain is the first step. But how do you apply those ideas and turn them into reality?

The first step is to stop looking at your internal and external suppliers separately or differently. You must begin by creating your value network map for each service to understand its value components by defining its scope and boundaries, determining roles and participants, identifying transactions and deliverables and sequencing the transactions. An IT Value Map looks somewhat different to Michael Porter's description of them. Given his manufacturing perspective, he saw the value stages as taking raw materials and transforming them, through the capabilities of the provider, into something that had greater value than the sum of the raw materials. In the IT Value Map, it may sometimes operate this way, but more often the Value Map will represent 'layers of value' that are built upon one another. In its simplest form, you can think of an IT Value Map as:

A Business Transaction *enabled through*

An Application *enabled through*

An Application Architecture (application servers, middleware components) *enabled through*

A Database Architecture *enabled through*

A Server Architecture *enabled through*

An Internal Network Architecture *enabled through*

An External Network Architecture

In most cases, each of these is itself enabled through other internal or external service providers, equipment providers, support providers, etc. The ultimate value that the customer receives through the enabled business transaction is actually the sum of each of these value-adding service components layered upon one another. While each IT service will likely follow some form of this generic pattern, the actual Value Map for the service will be specific and explicit.

The value components are logical constructs and do not necessarily represent suppliers. A single supplier may provide many layers of added value to the service. Therefore, the next step is to identify the various suppliers (who may be internal or external) and the value components that they are responsible for providing. You must also identify any dependencies that may exist, in order for them to deliver their added value, and identify whether those dependencies are internal or external to that supplier. Once you have mapped the value components to the various suppliers responsible for delivering them and associated those with the internal and external dependencies and parameters that will dictate delivery rate and risk, you will have established your supply chain.

Once you have established your supply chain in this fashion, you will have created a 'delivery system' for each service, which you can then monitor from the perspective of the continued ability of your suppliers to deliver their value components as a part of this system. Viewing these layered value components as a system will enable you to see any changes to the delivery capability in the context of the overall value to be delivered. This viewpoint, however, will cause a fundamental shift in how both internal delivery teams and external suppliers are managed.

Rather than the traditional approaches, in which functional teams are managed in the context of discreet objectives or some other static measure, and in which external suppliers are managed via rigid Service Level Agreements (SLAs), the supply-chain management capability of the Quantum IT organization will look more like a train dispatching center. The train dispatchers do not manage each train in isolation, based solely on their specific cargo or destination. Instead, they manage a system comprising fixed resources (the tracks, stations, and other infrastructure components) and a set of dynamic resources that deliver discrete value through the systems (the trains and their cargo or passengers). They stop trains, slow them, reassign tracks, and do whatever is necessary to protect the system and, by doing so, deliver the value at all levels of the system as consistently and reliably as possible.

This holistic approach to managing your supply chain will require different roles, different attitudes, and different skills. But this approach cannot simply be mandated. If the players do not understand the systemic nature of the supply chain, then they will simply see this type of management as bureaucracy. Likewise, if those put in charge of managing the supply-chain system fail to see their role as protectors and guardians of the system, then they will be at risk of believing that they hold power for its own sake. Rather than managing the system for the purpose of delivering through the supply chain the greatest amount of value possible, they will manage it to satisfy whatever they perceive to be the greatest cause or need. Whether benign or malevolent, it will have missed the mark and will ultimately fail in delivering the value it was meant to deliver and protect.

To effectively establish and manage this systemic supply chain, IT leaders must first and foremost utilize it as the primary means by which they manage and communicate. Conversations, planning, and management activities must all be centered around the core concepts of customers and how value is delivered to them through the supply chain. It must be made clear that if one part of the supply chain fails to deliver value, then the entire system has failed and all parts of the system are therefore damaged and culpable. It must be recognized that there is no such thing as an independent action. All actions within one part of the system will have an impact and effect on other parts of the system – even if they are not recognized immediately. The system must not be merely a metaphor for how value is created and delivered. It must be the reality of how the entire organization is managed.

New traits and new skills for a new age

As you've probably realized by now, this transition into the Quantum Age of IT is not a trivial one. It will require fundamental shifts in all aspects of how the IT function is organized and operated. It will require fundamental shifts in how IT leaders manage. It will require fundamental shifts in how IT professionals at all levels of the organization see themselves. The transition from manufacturer to retailer will be highly disruptive. The need to move away from being 'Walstrom' to choosing to be either a Strategic Innovator or a Strategic Sourcer will require some difficult decisions that fundamentally alter some of the foundational approaches to operating an IT organization.

In short, the Quantum Age will require a new set of organizational traits and a new set of individual skills.

There is good news. These traits and skills are not black magic. They are rooted in long-standing business disciplines and will be readily accessible and familiar to most IT professionals. At the same time, however, these traits and skills are not those that have historically been recognized and rewarded in IT organizations. Because of the ever-increasing complexity of the technology that IT organizations have been required to support, it has been the technical skills that have been most highly regarded. Many people will see the organizational traits and professional skills that will be critical in the Quantum Age as 'soft skills,' as intangible and 'nice to have,' but not essential to running an IT organization.

But they will be dead wrong.

The future of the IT organization lies in the development of these organizational traits and in the mastery of these skills. Unlike technical skills, which have a limited shelf life and must be constantly refreshed, these organizational traits and professional skills represent the development a new IT capability. A capability that is at once dynamic and optimized. One that it is not based on a limited technical footprint, but one that is instead built around dynamically meeting unforeseen customer demand and need. It is through the development of these traits and in the mastery of these skills that the IT organization will be transformed and will enter the Quantum Age.

Chapter 4 key points

Many IT organizations are finally reaching what feels like a point of stability. The last thing we want is more change. But the market is shifting beneath our feet. We can either resist the changes or we can adapt. There is really no choice. We must adapt. We must go from being manufactures to retailers.

Here are the key points you should remember from this chapter:

- While we haven't recognized it, the shift from a manufacturing paradigm to a retail one has been happening for some time.
- This explains a lot of the challenges we've had with our customers – we've been operating like manufacturers, but they see us retailers.
- To succeed in a retail paradigm, you need to develop new capabilities: supply-chain management, product management, and merchandising and customer experience management.
- Our customers don't want us to be a 'broker' of IT services – they want us to understand the value they seek and deliver it to them.
- The heart of supply-chain management is recognizing how value is created through the value network.
- In order to effectively manage complex supply chains and value networks, you must understand and apply systems thinking.

PART III

THE FIVE TRAITS OF THE QUANTUM IT ORGANIZATION

CHAPTER 5: NEW ORGANIZATIONAL TRAITS FOR A NEW AGE

My father was born in the Boyle Heights section of East Los Angeles. The life of his childhood was difficult. And dangerous. There was a definitive culture of his neighborhood that dictated the skills and attitudes that you needed to survive. There were rules in this culture. Most of them were unstated, but they were rules nonetheless. Never let anyone see weakness. Respect belonged to the guy with the biggest stick. Keep your head down and worry about yourself. If someone messes with you, give it right back to them – don't let anyone think that they can mess with you and get away with it.

It was a tough way to grow up and many of his family members and friends fell victim to it. But thankfully for my entire family, he got out. Through a safe haven called the Variety Boys Club (now known as the Variety Boys & Girls Club), he was able to separate himself from the worst of what his neighborhood and its culture offered. As a young boy, my father exhibited all of the traits that his culture demanded. He was fiercely independent. At the age of six, he would take a public bus and travel, by himself, across town to run away to the Boys Club, where they had a library with games and books. At even the youngest age, he projected a 'don't mess with me' attitude. And it served him well.

As he spent time at the Boys Club and at his eventual job at the city library, things began to change. Through his voracious appetite for reading, he was exposed to new ideas and new worldviews. He was able to see the world through a lens that was different to the one his neighborhood culture offered. It expanded his concept of what was possible in his own life and planted the idea that the characteristics and traits so prevalent in his corner of the world were not necessarily universal.

Eventually, this would lead him out of East Los Angeles.

He joined the Los Angeles County Sheriff's Department and began what would become a career of over 30 years. He retired at the rank of lieutenant after leading an amazing array of the most prestigious units in the department: the gang task force, homicide, and SWAT (known as the Special Enforcement Bureau within the Department), among many others. He was part of joint task forces with other police departments and federal agencies such as the FBI. He was a key part of the team coordinating potential emergency response actions for the 1984 Olympics and for the 1994 World Cup. Upon his retirement from the department, he went on to join the leadership team of a major entertainment company's security operations group and presently sits on the Board of Directors of the highly prestigious Joint Powers Act Crime Lab.

Beyond being immensely proud of my father, why have I shared his story with you? Because he is symbolic of the transition that must occur both individually and organizationally within IT organizations. It is often said that a 'leopard cannot change his spots.' That is meant to say that a person cannot change the core of their being – of who they really are as a person. That may be true, but I believe that, in reality, that inner core is actually very small. It may be the fount of our being, but much of what we then proceed to ascribe to that core is, in fact, traits which are merely artifacts of the culture in which we live. My father began his life embodying a set of traits that served him in that time: fierce independence, a 'don't mess with me' attitude, projecting unflinching strength. But as you contemplate his career as I described it, do you believe that those same traits would have led him to the success he found?

Beginning in his early days in the Boys Club, he was beginning to learn a new set of traits. Traits such as a commitment to lifelong learning, teamwork, empathy, and the ability to inspire others. It is these traits that would fuel his career success. Undoubtedly, his earlier traits would still prove useful at times in the field. But it was his 'new traits' that enabled him to build teams, to inspire them to follow in uncertain circumstances, to forge alliances across the political minefields of interdepartmental task forces, and to come through his career as a highly respected member of the law enforcement community.

As humans – and particularly as organizations – we often take the easy way out. We say that people cannot change. We talk about cultures as if they are indelible edifices that will never be altered. But, in fact, humans have an almost infinite capacity for self-transformation and a culture is a dynamic, living thing that is continually shaped by the people that embody it.

As we enter the Quantum Age, IT organizations must develop and adopt five new traits that will define their success going forward. The purpose of my father's story is to simply head off the automatic reaction that you might have – that the organization cannot change. It serves as a warning not to let what is perhaps an unstated belief seep into your subconscious: that the IT organization is a culture that will not be altered. It can be and it must be. In fact, the only thing that can stop it from changing is a belief that it cannot.

On the other hand, all it really takes to change the culture of your organization and to embody the five traits of the Quantum IT organization is a belief that it is possible. My father's story is one that I go to often in my own life when I need a reminder that change is always possible; when I need to remember that we are always in control of our own destiny. It is the foundation for why I believe that IT organizations can make this transition. We must simply believe it to be so.

The design of your culture

Every organization has a culture. But almost none of them were explicitly created. They just happen. Slowly, over time, molded bit by bit by each leader who took his or her turn – and by every person they ever hired.

This is particularly true of IT organizations.

As we explored in the first chapter, the IT organization happened almost by accident and has been moving at warp speed ever since. It was not deliberately conceived. It was not designed. No one ever contemplated the optimal cultural footing for an organization like IT. In fact, until the last few years few people even talked in terms of there being a culture in IT at all. For generations, IT has been looked at as a collection of technical geeks, barely part of the larger organization at all – let alone having a distinct culture of their own. But as IT organizations grew over time, as they grew larger, as they grew more complex – a distinct culture developed uniquely within every IT organization.

In many ways, most IT organizations share some common cultural elements. There is a natural cadence to the way IT people think and in how they interact. There are attitudes and viewpoints that we largely share and which bind us together. At the same time, however, every culture is unique. The culture of your IT organization is first and foremost influenced by the culture of the larger organization. They are not the same, but many of the core values of the IT culture will be inherited from the larger culture. In the modern enterprise, IT organizations are often cobbled together from acquisitions and mergers, injecting additional cultural cues.

All of these influences create a distinct culture. You need to recognize that your culture exists and that it can work for you or against you. The question is whether or not your culture can sustain the changes that are required as we enter this new age. You must understand and address this explicitly.

The transition to the Quantum Age requires fundamental shifts in almost everything that makes up the modern IT organization. This fundamentally means that the culture of your IT organization will be shifting – whether you like it or not. But while you can see this as something scary, it is also a great opportunity to shape the culture of the organization explicitly so that the culture works for you and for your efforts to achieve your objectives.

Perhaps for the first time in the history of our industry, we have the opportunity to explicitly contemplate and design our culture in a way that genuinely serves our needs. The disruption that the Quantum Age brings creates an opportunity to break through 'the way we've always done things' and create the culture that we need to take us into a new future.

The problem with talking about culture is that it feels abstract. What is a culture anyway? If you were put on the spot, could you describe yours? Would the person in the next office or cubicle describe it in the same way? Culture can mean a lot of things. It conveys a way of thinking. It represents a set of values. It is embodied in a set of traits or characteristics that are shared by those who live within the culture. Many aspects of your current culture are good. At our core, IT people are good people who want to serve their customers and make them happy. But over time, IT organizations have developed a set of characteristics which have become a barrier to those core values. Those are the parts of the culture that must change if you are to remain relevant in the coming era.

That is what this part of the book is about: defining the five traits that will serve as the building blocks of the organizational culture that you will design to take your organization into the Quantum Age.

What was wrong with our old traits?

As we begin to discuss the 'new traits' for the Quantum Age, it may bring forth a fair question: what was wrong with our old traits? The answer is, probably nothing. They were most likely appropriate for the time and era in which they were created. But just as my father needed to adopt new traits as his environment and needs changed, IT organizations must adopt new traits as the world changes and the demands on the IT organization evolve with it.

Those traits that were once so well suited now begin to work against the organization rather than for it.

So while there was nothing inherently wrong with our existing traits, we have to recognize that they will work against us if we do not evolve them. That means that we must begin by understanding how our existing traits work against us so that we can rationally contemplate and then communicate the need for change.

If we think of the evolution of the IT function, it is easy to see why our old traits developed as they did. Computers were originally developed to deal with highly complex and often mundane tasks of calculation. As we saw in *Chapter 1*, the modern computing environment in which technology is woven into the fabric of all aspects of life is actually a very new development. Until the end of the 20th century, virtually all applications of technology came down to some form of complex calculation of a processing function. As a result, the traits that came to embody the IT function were built around these needs. Traits such as precision, stability, and the ability to accurately understand and translate very specific requirements were paramount.

There was little value ascribed to 'understanding' the customer. IT was not about innovation. It was about automation. The customer knew what calculation or processing needed to occur. They could describe it in precise detail. What they valued was that IT could grasp what they explained and then translate it to do 'the magic' that was required to automate that process or calculation. Once that was done, all they needed was for it to work, for it to be something that they could count on. The mainframe and midrange computing environments were perfect tools for this task. Precision and stability were designed into the platform. It required people to operate it like a piece of machinery. And so the IT function developed around these traits.

As the era of personal computing evolved in the late 1980s and the 1990s, it began to put pressure on these traits. Precision and stability began to translate into rigidity and slowness. As the complexity that was managed within the walls of a single platform burst out into a distributed environment, the simple order of running a 'computing machine' proved insufficient. Yet despite all of the changes that have occurred, the traits of the IT organization have fundamentally persisted. And they are now working against the needs of the modern IT organization.

Creating new mental models

There is another reason to explicitly identify these five organizational traits, and that is to help in reframing the mental models that guide much of how IT organizations operate. Whether you realize it or not, much of everything that we think, decide upon, and do as humans is based on our mental models. Mental models are complex sets of instructions that we naturally create to help us make sense of our world and to manage the barrage of information that we are bombarded with on a daily basis. Overall, having mental models is a good thing. They help us be productive and effective. But because they are one of the primary mechanisms we use to cope with our daily existence, we tend to protect them and allow them to operate under the surface. Which means that we fail to recognize that they are there at all and therefore never change them. When the real world begins to change around us, but our mental models don't, they begin to work against us.

Our current operational traits are embedded into these mental models. Whenever we talk about 'computer operations,' we are reinforcing the mental model of 'operating a machine.' When we use the organizational paradigms of 'application development' and 'infrastructure' we reinforce the mental models of a slow, linear manufacturing process whereby a product is designed and developed by one team and then given to another to operate. Whenever we complain about our customer's inability to 'clearly define their requirements' we reinforce the mental model of IT as the automator rather than the innovator.

Our existing traits and the mental models that we have built around them create what Peter Senge calls a balancing feedback process. This is a process which essentially seeks stability. As such, it creates resistance to anything that will upset the status quo. These traits and mental models are deeply seated into the identity of nearly every IT organization and every IT professional. When they are threatened by any effort that will fundamentally shift that identity, these balancing feedback processes kick in and attempt to correct it. It is subtle, but it is what fundamentally leads to the attitudes that become prevalent when change is introduced. Attitudes like 'this is how we've always done it,' or 'we've already tried that here and it didn't work,' or 'we're different and what worked elsewhere won't work here' are reflections of this balancing feedback system at work.

In ways visible and hidden, there is a natural instinct to protect our identity. And that instinct is fierce. It is why change efforts that simply introduce something new and instruct people to follow a new process or procedure are rarely successful. Unless the change is trivial and does not challenge our identity, we will subconsciously rise up to protect the status quo. It is why, in order to successfully transform our organizations and enter the Quantum Age, we must change our mental models.

By explicitly identifying these five organizational traits and utilizing them as we reshape our organizational culture, we will begin also to reshape those mental models that guide how we operate on a daily basis. Failing to change the mental models that underpin how you and your teams work means that you will simply be rearranging the chairs on the deck of the ship – but that the ship will still be going in the same direction.

The journey to change your organizational traits

Excellence is not a destination; it is a continuous journey that never ends.

Brian Tracy

Reshaping your mental models and changing the fundamental traits that underpin your IT organization is not a trivial matter. It represents a fundamental transformation of your organization. As with the pursuit of excellence, the transformation into a Quantum Age organization is not a destination. It too is a journey. It is a journey to change the culture of IT in the sense of changing IT's sense of identity and organizational worth. The core of our culture will remain, but how we look at ourselves via our mental models and the traits that we embody will change. That is not as impossible as it might sound, but it requires its own type of discipline and an explicit effort to make it happen.

A culture is a dynamic, living system that is, by its very nature, changeable. But change cannot be forced from the outside in. It must happen from the inside out. A culture only changes from within and only when it is driven to by some force bigger than itself. In his book *The Fifth Discipline*, Peter Senge identifies that there are essentially only two drivers for this type of transformation when he writes, "There are two sources of energy that can motivate organizations: fear and aspirations."

He describes this in the context of a need for a shared vision that can drive an organization forward. He goes on to state that while both fear and aspiration can motivate an organization, fear is often more temporary and transient because as soon as the fear passes, so too does the will to change. In the case of IT organizations, fear will be a significant motivator. Almost everyone is beginning to recognize the threat to the historical model of IT. But there will be a reprieve. As economics improve and as an organization begins to find some initial, incremental success through their transformational efforts, it will appear that things are getting better and getting back to normal. And the motivation for change will wane. But as we've discovered in the first two parts of this book, there is a fundamental shift occurring and any relief will be temporary.

As an IT leader, you must be willing to go beyond fear. You must create a shared, aspirational vision for what your IT organization can and must become. (And if you don't think of yourself as an IT leader, you need to start, as we'll discuss in Chapter 10.) You must commit yourself to this journey. You must commit to seeing your organization through this transformation and be prepared to execute an explicit plan to make it happen.

Changing your culture and developing these organizational traits will be unlike any technology project you have ever implemented. You cannot 'implement' these traits. You will be required to embark on a highly disciplined journey to develop these traits and change your culture. The specifics of how to execute this kind of a change program is beyond the scope of this book and there are several great works already available on the subject. But there are a few key points that you must be aware of that are specific to IT organizations.

A shared aspirational vision

The need for a concrete, aspirational vision cannot be overstated. In far too many situations, IT organizations have almost no sense whatsoever of who they are as an organization and, more importantly, who they seek to become. IT organizations just do. A glance at most IT 'strategic plans' will find nothing more than a collection of short-term projects. There is a misconception that IT professionals do not respond to typical motivators. Fill the office refrigerator with Red Bull and leave them alone. But IT professionals are perhaps more motivated than most by the promise of a future powered by the technology we build, deploy, and support. IT professionals desperately want to be seen as an integral part of their companies and to be recognized for their contributions. A truly aspirational vision is an incredibly powerful tool that is often entirely missing from IT organizations.

5: New Organizational Traits for a New Age

Dump the 'touchy-feely'

While IT professionals want to be part of something bigger than themselves and will respond to an aspirational vision, we are still technical in our nature. As a result, we do not often respond well to the typical 'touchy-feely' parts of organizational change efforts. Rather than a bunch of silly exercises, you need to find a way to help your teams embed the core attributes of organizational change directly into their efforts. They need to practice challenging assumptions, active and open inquiry, and true engagement and enablement. Finally, you must recognize that this needs to be cascaded throughout the organization. Part III of Peter Senge's *The Fifth Discipline* and Chip and Dan Heath's *Switch* provide great details on how to make this happen.

Help them focus on 'what'

If IT folks have one attribute that is somewhat unique to our industry, it is our love of playing with the shiny new toy. While I hate to paint all IT people with the same brush, the reality is that most IT professionals are gadget people. We love new technology and tend to flock from trend to trend, always eager to explore the 'latest and greatest.' The challenge is that this can often lead us to a posture of 'ready, fire, aim.' As you embark on this journey, the most important question in your arsenal will be 'what?' As IT folks, we are programmed to ask 'how?' But as the first step in changing our mental models, we need to learn that we must begin by asking 'what?' What are we trying to accomplish? What does our desired end-state look like? What is broken that is stopping us from realizing that today? What are the specific objectives we hope to achieve? Only after the 'whats' have been clearly articulated can we go on to ask how to solve the problem that we now clearly understand.

Give them the freedom to fail

IT people hate failure. Given our historical mental models, with our identity associated with stability and precision, failure is simply not an option. But as you seek to change the culture of your organization to adopt these new traits, you must recognize that you are trying to teach yourself and your teams a new way of interacting and learning. Key to this process will be giving yourself and your teams the freedom to fail. It is only in trying something new – and often in that something failing – that we truly learn. You can sit through a thousand training classes. But until you actually try something, you won't learn it. Shared exploration and knowing that much of what your teams attempt will fail (or at least not succeed fully) will be the surest way to break down the barriers and inertia of the way things have always been done and pave the way for the transformation you seek.

People often react viscerally when I tell them that they need to learn to fail, when I challenge them to give their teams the freedom to fail. The word 'failure' carries such stigma that the reaction is almost always immediate. But we are not talking about the abject, lose-your-job kind of failure here. In fact, it is just the opposite. This 'freedom to fail' is about rapidly trying out new things, figuring out what's working and what's not, correcting and moving forward. It could be something as simple as putting in a new process, without worrying if it's perfect, and then gauging the results. If it doesn't achieve what you were hoping for, adjust it or throw it away and try again – without any stigma associated.

Are you willing to accept that you must change the culture of your IT organization and embark on a journey to embed a new set of traits? Are you prepared to challenge the mental models that keep you in the status quo? That is the journey ahead of you. Are you ready to take this step forward?

The five traits of the Quantum IT organization

If you're still reading this book, you've just stepped over the threshold. You've been told of the dangers facing your organization and that a great change from within must take place. You understand that you are embarking on a journey that will fundamentally alter the way that your entire organization operates and you've accepted the responsibility to help your organization see it through.

Here, then, is the journey that you will be taking. You will lead your organization in the development of the five traits of the Quantum Age and become:

A Learning Organization

A Disciplined Organization

A Transparent Organization

An Intimate Organization

A Dynamic Organization.

We will discuss what each of these means over the next four chapters, but they may seem simple and obvious at this point. They are. But what makes them unique is not the traits themselves, but rather that these traits become the defining characteristic of the IT organization of the Quantum Age. Viewed from that perspective, it is notable that the traits of precision and stability and translation are not there. Precision and stability are key components of being a disciplined organization, but, significantly, they are not defining or predominant. Likewise, the trait of being skilled in translation is gone, replaced by the much more difficult and involved traits of transparency and intimacy. These five traits, while almost certainly latent within your organization to varying degrees, take on a new meaning when they become defining. As the defining traits of the IT organization, they will represent a fundamentally different identity and sense of organizational value. They will fundamentally alter the foundation of the relationship between IT and its customers and it will require a substantially different skill set within the team of IT professionals that make up the IT organization (which is what Part IV of this book is about.)

The remaining chapters in Part III will explore each of these five traits in detail. We will define what it means to embody this trait and give real-world examples of IT organizations that are already moving down this road. You will learn how this trait will fundamentally change the way your IT organization must operate and view its role. Finally, you will get tangible and real-world examples of how to begin breaking down mental models and other barriers and begin embedding each of these traits into the fabric of your organizational culture.

The road will, at times, be scary. Fundamental shifts like this bring with them much fear. You will never get everything right out the gate. There will be fits and starts. There will be failures and triumphs. There are no guarantees. But I am sure of two things. First, this change is coming and is going to happen whether we believe in it or want it or not. Second, for those brave enough to step out and lead their IT organization through this change, it will be the most exciting time that we've ever seen in our industry.

I am glad that you have decided to go on this journey. You are going to be a part of something big, something meaningful. You are going to change the world of IT and help to lead your organization into the Quantum Age.

Let's do it.

Chapter 5 key points

We often talk about cultures and organizations as immutable edifices that cannot change. But the truth is that, as both people and organizations, we have an almost infinite capacity for transformation. To enter the Quantum Age, IT organizations will need to adapt and evolve. You will need to develop five specific traits. It will be hard, but more than anything it will simply require a belief that it is possible.

Here are the key points you should remember from this chapter:

- You need to acknowledge that IT organizations have a distinct culture and that it can work both for and against you.
- The transition to the Quantum Age will result in a cultural shift.
- Our 'old traits' were fine for our past, but they are now working against us as we move into the Quantum Age.

- Our existing mental models anchor us to our past and to the way 'we've always done things' – we need to change them if we are to successfully move our organizations.

- The transition into the Quantum Age is not a destination – it is a journey to change the culture of the IT organization.

- To succeed, you must execute an organizational change program that creates a shared aspirational vision, avoids being 'touchy-feely,' focuses on the 'what,' and offers your team the 'freedom to fail.'

CHAPTER 6: A TICKET TO THE DANCE: CREATING A LEARNING AND DISCIPLINED ORGANIZATION

When Joel Manfredo joined the County of Orange, California as CTO he found a lot of good people – and a lot of chaos. At the time, in addition to all the normal operational work involved in running a $60 million service delivery business, there were 77 active projects and no priorities. From an operational perspective, employees were constantly being redirected, sometimes multiple times daily, based on 'who called last.' His job was to create order out of the chaos – and to begin the journey to take the County of Orange into the Quantum Age.

He instinctively knew that his first priority was to change the perspectives of his team. "People are constrained in their thought by their experience. If they haven't done it before, it doesn't exist," Joel said. There was this prevailing sense that Joel's efforts were just another thing that would eventually pass without having any meaningful impact. They'd seen it all before. They knew that if they just waited it out long enough, this too would pass.

Were they wrong?

Joel began by focusing on a set of tactical activities that would have an immediate, positive improvement in service. He was focused and unrelenting. He knew that the expectations were stacked against him both from inside his organization and with his customers. He knew that these initial efforts were not going to fix the problem. But his focus was less on the activities themselves and more on teaching his team to expect that change was possible – to embrace change and to understand how to continually pursue improvement.

But he did more than merely focus on the tactical problems. He began focusing on his people themselves. He conducted a series of personal assessments and workshops and then established a monthly session to help members of his team understand personalities and learn how to communicate with one another. Many on his team were undoubtedly rolling their eyes at all of this 'soft stuff,' particularly when there were frustrated customers expecting things to get better.

Joel persisted. Eventually, he broke through. His teams began to learn how to communicate. Really communicate. They began to engage in what Senge refers to as 'dialogue.' They were doing more than just 'sharing status' and politely waiting their turn to talk. They were actively listening to each other. They were challenging their own assumptions. Working together they created strategies and kicked off efforts that solved the problems that they'd identified together.

Whether they knew it or not, out of the chaos he inherited, Joel was helping his team evolve into a 'learning organization' and laying the foundation to create a truly 'disciplined organization.'

The credibility gap

Doing things well. Doing things reliably. Doing things consistently. These are not cool and sexy.

This is kind of the IT equivalent of being the polite, studious teenage boy – you know, the one that never gets the girl. Even in the world of IT, we all want to be the 'bad boy,' the 'rock star,' or the star athlete. We want to work on the cool and exciting projects. We want to do things that get the attention and the adoration. Of course, given the common personality of most IT folks, we pretend that we don't like the attention. Yet we are naturally drawn to those projects that are somehow cool and sexy (at least as cool and sexy as a technology project can be!).

This is why, every year, IT organizations all over the world fill their project portfolios full of new projects that will deploy the latest and coolest new whatever. Every year, we purchase a veritable raft of 'shiny new toys.' But what about all of the projects that have already been completed? Like last year's Christmas toys, they're no longer fun and cool. They're now just part of 'normal operations.' And so when those things are not working quite right, when they're operating inefficiently, when they're overly bureaucratic, well, that can wait, right? IT organizations rarely put in the time and effort that is really needed to do the hard work of doing things right.

There is a perception that there is too little capacity of IT resources against too much demand from our customers to invest in doing things right and fixing these inefficiencies. It is seen as a low-leverage activity that has limited or at least an invisible return on investment. So organizations make token efforts, but never fully commit to doing what is necessary to create the kind of organization that delivers consistently and reliably.

The problem with this is that it comes with a very high price tag in the form of lost credibility.

Every time the IT organization fails to deliver services in a consistent and reliable fashion, the faith that our customers have in us gets depleted. Frankly, most IT organizations are now operating on credit. All credibility is lost and they're working on borrowed time. This is why shadow IT organizations are created. It's why customers bypass IT and go straight to some form of a software-as-a-service provider. It's why every proposal, every budget request, no matter how small or insignificant, is challenged.

But the price is even greater than this. This loss of credibility means that the IT organization has lost or severely limited its role as a trusted adviser to its customers. When people complain about IT being commoditized, it is a direct reflection of this lost credibility. Where there is no trust, there is no value. So when IT leaders (remember, that's you) decide that they want to make things better and find the courage to approach customers with new ideas to become more strategic and proactive, they are met with skepticism or are outright rejected.

Whether they say it or not, the customer is thinking, "Great, you want to be strategic. How about you just keep our systems running first."

The unfortunate byproduct is that you walk away from that exchange frustrated and demoralized – and much less likely to go down that road again. So the cycle continues and deepens. And so it has gone in IT organizations for as long as most of us can remember.

The cycle needs to be broken.

Your ticket to the dance

Before change can happen, before you can have that strategic conversation, you need to close this credibility gap. While this may rub you wrong, the truth is that you need to earn the right to have that conversation. You need to demonstrate that you can deliver your services effectively, efficiently, and consistently before your customer is going to be willing to genuinely have that strategic conversation.

It's not that they don't want to have that conversation. In fact, they desperately want to have it. They're dying to have it. But they don't want to waste their time talking about something that is probably not going to happen. You're asking for an investment from them. You're asking them to invest their time and their energy. And they're not confident that it's an investment that will give them a return.

So they keep the conversation on safe ground. They remain focused on the things that they feel will produce a return: small improvements, incremental upgrades, reducing costs. But what they really want is to be able to go to the next level. They want to have that conversation and know that it can really happen.

They want you to come to the dance. But you need a ticket.

Your ticket to the dance is to create an organization that can deliver its services the right way, every day. Over time, you will demonstrate that your organization can be counted on. That you will deliver the services you've promised, as you've promised, every time. That consistency and reliability will close the credibility gap and rebuild the trust between you and your customers.

The challenge is that you cannot mandate or decree an organization like this into existence. Simply declaring that your organization will be 'world class' will not do it. You cannot create this kind of organization by giving motivational speeches and hanging some posters.

Why is creating this kind of consistent and predictable organization hard in the first place? Mostly because in large organizations there are too many moving parts. There are too many specialized functions with too many weak links between them. There are too many competing priorities and incentives. There are too many fiefdoms and too many undercurrents that work against the organization from the inside out.

There is only one way to change this and create the kind of organization that can turn the tide. You need to change the dynamic. That is what creating a learning organization is all about. Creating a learning organization lays the foundation for changing how teams work and interact. It is from that foundation that you can then build a highly disciplined organization. (But, fair warning: this type of discipline may not be what you're thinking about. We'll get to that in a moment.)

So the ticket to the dance, the path to closing the credibility gap and rebuilding trust, is to fundamentally change the way you view how you work by turning your IT organization into a learning and highly disciplined organization.

What it means to be a learning organization

The term 'learning organization' was popularized by Peter Senge in the book *The Fifth Discipline*, which I have already referenced extensively. His book is an entire work on the basic components and constructs of what it means to become a learning organization. I will not attempt to duplicate and condense that extensive work here, but there are some important points that must be understood.

6: A Ticket to the Dance

In the book, Senge discusses the trepidation with which they adopted the term in the first place. They believed it was likely that the term would become a 'fad' and lose its true, deeper meaning. Largely, they were right. Today, the term 'learning organization' is used commonly. But few people apply the discipline of practice that should accompany it and instead reduce it to a platitude. The greatest loss is that most people have now applied a passive point of view to the concept of a learning organization. In this mindset, simply having a formal educational and professional-development program should do the trick. But this is a complete misapplication of the intent.

Being a learning organization is not a passive posture. Being a learning organization is action-oriented.

First and foremost, a learning organization is one that recognizes that everything is interconnected. That we cannot solve problems in isolation, pretending that they are not connected as part of a larger whole – what Senge calls a system. He calls this view 'systems thinking' and simply means that as we work to improve things we must both be aware of how other components of the system impact the problem we are trying to solve and be aware of the impact of any change to the system on the other components. The power in this approach is that instills a recognition that we are all in this together.

What would happen if everyone in IT always looked at the whole of the situation? If we always considered the impact that our actions had on others in the organization and our ability to deliver services as an integrated team? If, when trying to solve problems, we stopped finger-pointing and each recognized our contribution to the failure? At its core, creating a learning organization is rooted in the concepts of responsibility and accountability. It is about education, but it is about everyone in the organization taking responsibility for educating themselves about how their actions and decisions impact others and the ability of the organization to fulfill its purpose.

A learning organization is one in which all members of the organization feel a deep accountability to the rest of the organization. There is no room for a 'not my job' attitude in a learning organization. There is an individual accountability to expose your assumptions because you understand that unstated assumptions are the root of miscommunication and misunderstanding. There is an individual responsibility to accept your own fault and failure so that you can give others the permission to expose theirs – thereby creating an environment in which you can mutually learn from each other's mistakes – and find solutions that work for both of you.

There is more to it, of course. Senge actually covers five disciplines of a learning organization: systems thinking, shared vision, personal mastery, mental models, and team learning. These disciplines are each constructs that enable an organization to break down barriers and build dynamic cohesion in which everyone is able to simultaneously pursue their objectives while doing so in the context of the overall goals of the organization. In their totality, they create what in IT circles we tend to call an 'adaptive organization.'

Whatever we call it, here is the takeaway: a learning organization is not about 'education' per se. A learning organization is one where every member of the organization shares a vision of what they are trying to achieve and accepts the personal accountability to challenge anything – within themselves or others – that will prevent the organization from achieving it. It is about commitment. It is about personal accountability. And it is about action.

The Ritz-Carlton is famous for its dedication to service and to the customer experience. What is not often recognized is that it is also a terrific example of what it means to be a true learning organization. Every single employee within the company, from senior executives to housekeeping staff, is authorized to spend up to $2,000 to solve a guest's problem and make them happy. But this is more than just a policy. With it comes responsibility. Every member of the Ritz-Carlton team is expected to take ownership of a guest's problem if they are the first to encounter it. There is no passing the buck. If a guest approaches them with a problem, it becomes their problem until it is solved or until someone takes it from them. They understand that no matter what their role, they all share a common mission – to serve the guest and make their experience as fantastic as possible. Even after the problem has been resolved, their responsibilities are not over. Every issue, every action is fed into a massive data stream to ensure that the organization can identify blind spots and opportunities, eliminate or leverage them, and continue thrilling their guests.

That is a learning organization.

It also demonstrates what true discipline looks like. Did you see it?

Why a robot is NOT disciplined

The Industrial Revolution did the world a disservice in one great sense. The rise of the modern, hierarchical business organization required that the business operate like a machine. The industrial barons built machines and assembly lines that worked reliably, consistently producing products on a predictable schedule. They needed their people to work the same way. So they instilled a sense of forced discipline to make sure that everyone did things the same way, every time. This represented a major departure from the way that people had worked beforehand. It was the beginning of a long retraining process to turn people into predictable, controllable resources. And it forever changed the meaning of the word 'discipline.' It is a legacy that persists today in almost all facets of life.

The word discipline actually comes from the Latin root *disciplina*, which means instruction or knowledge. True discipline is not about following the rules. It is about training yourself to act in a controlled and consistent fashion, even in challenging and changing circumstances. But that requires much more than merely following the rules. It requires intellect, practice, and creativity.

If we think about the preindustrial workforce, most people worked in agriculture or as tradesmen. Both of these required enormous discipline. In most cases, the only rules were those that were self-imposed by the worker himself. He understood what he was trying to accomplish and, through apprenticeship, he learned the habits and skills that were required to do it. But these habits and skills were not rote. People were not simply following some arbitrary rules. They were applying these habits and skills in an intelligent manner, using their discipline not as a cage, but as a tool that enabled them to get what they wanted.

In his book *Linchpin*, Seth Godin argues that this transition had lasting, negative effects on many aspects of our society – and that the time has come to change it. He states that the

6: A Ticket to the Dance

discipline of the industrial age has robbed us of our soul – at least at work – and that we need to fundamentally change how we view work. In fact, he goes as far as calling on everyone to become an 'artist.' It is his way of distinguishing between merely following the rules and creating something that is unique and powerful. He contends that starting with our earliest education and continuing through our entire professional lives, most of us are fed a steady diet of strict structure and mindless work. Even in the modern incarnation of the 'knowledge worker,' most of the work doesn't require the act of creation – it doesn't require art. We are taught to do what we are told.

In the movie *I, Robot*, a character played by Will Smith has a heavy disdain for the millions of robots that now handle the everyday tasks that people do not want to do themselves. The reason for his hate of the robots is because during a car accident a robot saved him – instead of saving a young girl. The logic was simple. The robot calculated that Will Smith's character had a better chance of survival and so, as it was programmed to do, it saved the victim that was more likely to live. Would you say that the robot had discipline? It was simply doing what it was programmed to do. No more. No less.

Most people will agree that a robot does not have discipline. It is programmed to perform tasks in a specific way. It has no choice. There is no discretion. It does what it is told. There are a lot of situations where this is good. In fact, it is perfect. Where a task requires no thought, no discretion, then a robot is the perfect fit for the job. The question, however, is why would we try to turn our most valuable 'asset' – our people – into robots?

When IT professionals talk about discipline, this is what they are normally trying to do. Of course, put in these terms, no one will admit to it. But when organizations embark on some form of an efficiency program or try to improve service, it almost always comes down to this: how can we make all of our people use the same process and follow the same rules, every time?

The phrase 'we need to increase discipline within our organization,' really means, 'we need everyone to act the same way.'

But why?

Is that what we really want? Of course not. Yet that is what our processes, policies, and bureaucracies are built to do. In his book *Breaking the Fear Barrier*, Tom Rieger tells the fictional story of Joe. Joe joins a new company and is eager to make things happen. He is driven. He is enthusiastic. He has ideas. But he runs smack into meaningless processes, policies, and bureaucracies that repeatedly slap him back into place. Finally, he is beaten down. He succumbs to the organizational inertia and simply begins to go through the motions. All of his creative energy is lost. He loses all incentive to make a difference, to produce value for the customer. He accepts that he cannot win the battle and so he allows himself to become the automaton that they wanted. But, deep down, he knows that it is not the right thing. He begins to become bitter as he feels his creative energy slip away.

Finally, Joe gets a new boss. She is willing to break through the barriers, to challenge assumptions, and she creates an aspirational vision for the impact that they can have if they work as a team. (Sounds a lot like a learning organization, doesn't it?) Rieger explains this from the perspective of how these edifices were built in the first place. His core message is that fear is the overriding driver for these behaviors. As people seek to protect and insulate themselves, they begin creating these organizational barriers. But while these processes, policies, and bureaucracies may appear to create a layer of protection through this sense of false discipline, what they are really doing is bottling up the creative energy, the powerful desire to have an impact that exists within the organization.

We need discipline in IT organizations. As we enter the Quantum Age, we need to become a highly disciplined organization. But we need real discipline.

True discipline implies thought, decisions, and discretion. It means having the training and knowledge necessary to be able to determine what is the right thing to do and then act on that decision accordingly – even in the face of significant pressure. The challenge is that creating this kind of true discipline is a lot harder than simply trying to get people to follow the rules. You can beat someone down until they finally agree simply to do what you say. But true discipline has to be grown. It cannot be imposed. It must come from within each of us.

There is another reason why creating a truly disciplined organization is hard. It requires a loss of control. Fake discipline is all about control. Rules are established on high and everyone else does what they're told. Those who set the rules have the control. But to create a disciplined organization, you have to let go of that need for control. Discipline comes from understanding the mission and then having the skills and training to do what is necessary to achieve it. Consistently. Reliably.

Which brings us to the final reason why creating a disciplined organization is hard. It requires training. But not the kind of training that most IT organizations do today. In most IT organizations, training has been reduced to a color-by-number exercise. Here are the process steps. Here is the software application. Do step one, followed by step two, and so on. But what is most often missing is the reason, the objective. Why are you asking them to do this? What is the ultimate outcome that you're seeking? What critical skills will they need to achieve that outcome?

Have you ever watched one of those historical action films? You know the type. Some small band of outcasts or underdogs of some type rise up to fight the evil establishment. There is always a montage scene where they show the uninitiated fighters being trained to become valiant warriors (who will, of course, overcome all odds to win the day!). Do you notice that they are never sitting in neat little rows listening to an instructor? What are they doing instead? They're practicing! They learn by doing. They learn why each of the skills they are learning is important and how and when they should be applied. They are learning how to work together, how to communicate silently, how to coordinate their efforts. Not so they can play it back like some recording, but so they can adapt and react in the heat of battle.

That's discipline.

Learning and discipline starts with you

Embodying the traits of the learning organization and the disciplined organization is both *difficult* and *crucial*. It is difficult because of the limited 'cool factor.' It is difficult because even if you excel, your customers will barely notice. After all, all you will really be doing is delivering on the promises you have already made to them.

But do you know who will notice? You. And every member of your team. They will begin to feel like things really can change. They will start to remember that being in IT can be a lot of fun and that they really can deliver excellent and amazing service every day. That they truly can delight their customers.

We discussed earlier that creating a learning and disciplined organization was the ticket to the dance with your customers. But there is another dance and another ticket you need. You also have to demonstrate to your team that all of this change and effort is worth it. They too need to believe that there is something of worth at the end of this road. They too need to believe that there is a return on their investment.

Becoming a learning and disciplined organization is difficult. Your efforts may go largely unnoticed by your customers. But this is foundational. Everything that comes after this will be built upon the foundation of these two traits. In fact, most significant failures within IT organizations can be traced right back to these two traits. It is almost always the inability to continually learn and adapt and the lack of true discipline that are the source of significant failures and breakdowns. But as you begin to become this type of organization, things will begin to change. Your teams will begin to believe – really believe. And that will translate into something palpable for your customers. And that is what you need to begin developing the remaining three traits.

But because making the investment and commitment to becoming a learning and disciplined organization is both so difficult and so crucial, there is only one place where it can start. It must start with you.

The greatest single barrier to any team, of any size, becoming a learning and disciplined organization is the disconnect that often occurs between what a leader says and what a leader does. In order to become a learning and disciplined organization you need to begin by 'walking the talk.' The common theme of becoming both a learning and a disciplined organization is the pushing of accountability and control to the individuals in your organization. But accepting that challenge brings a huge amount of perceived risk with it, especially given the history of organizations and the long track record of being beaten down. Are they going to be willing to step up and step out? Not without some proof that it's for real.

It is therefore critical that you go first. You must be willing to challenge your own assumptions. Publicly. And not in a contrived manner. Genuinely challenge them. Like the Ritz-Carlton, you must give your team visible and tangible tools that make it plain that they really are being given the opportunity and responsibility to become individually accountable. You must be prepared to accept failure as a natural part of the learning cycle. You must move away from the train-once-and-done mentality. You must give people the opportunity to be creative. You must give them the freedom to experiment and exercise their critical thinking skills. You need to let them become artists.

I wish that there was some magic bullet here and I could tell you that you could do all of this without any impact. But it is simply not true. This is not an excuse to let your service expectations disintegrate. But you have to understand and accept that this will be completely new (at least from a professional perspective) for most people. There will be a lot of trial and error – a lot of learning. There will be some painful points and you'll need to resist the urge to be reactive. You may want to take control and handle the situation. But you can't. You need to let your team work through the process.

It is the only way that they will become the learning and disciplined organization that you need them to become.

It may be painful, especially at the beginning. But the payoff is massive. You will go from having a team of automatons to having a team of energetic, critically thinking people who are committed to helping the organization achieve its goals. And they will have the skills, the training, and the relationships that they need to get it done.

Chapter 6 key points

The journey into the Quantum Age begins with a focus on two traits: learning and discipline. They are the building blocks and the place where most IT organizations must begin.

Here are the key points you should remember from this chapter:

- Because they aren't cool, fun, or sexy, we tend to put off those things that will improve our organizational efficiency, but this comes at a great cost – our credibility.

- This creates a credibility gap that must be closed if we are to move forward.
- You need a 'ticket to the dance' – the 'right' to have the strategic conversation.
- Being a learning organization is not a passive posture. Being a learning organization is action-oriented.
- The key to becoming a learning organization is to adopt 'systems thinking' – to see how everything is connected to the larger whole.
- Being a learning organization is not about education as much as it's about being personally accountable for continually improvement.
- True discipline is not about following the rules. It is about training yourself to act in a controlled and consistent fashion, even in challenging and changing circumstances.
- Becoming a learning and disciplined organization is not cool. Your efforts may go largely unnoticed by your customers. But this is foundational. Everything that comes after this will be built upon the foundation of these two traits.

CHAPTER 7: KEY PRINCIPLES OF THE LEARNING AND DISCIPLINED ORGANIZATION

The process of becoming a learning and disciplined organization is a never-ending one. You will never be done. Like all of the traits that we will explore, the traits of learning and discipline are a way of operating that will require constant reinforcement, reevaluation, and recommitment.

As you have probably already begun, it will involve your seeking out and adopting operational and process improvement frameworks such as ITIL, COBIT, CMMi, IT-CMF and Lean Six Sigma. But in adopting these frameworks, your commitment to becoming a learning and disciplined organization will demand that you look at these frameworks and approaches holistically and with an eye toward how they can help you achieve your strategic objectives. Gone will be the days of simply adopting a framework because it sounded like a good thing to do. A reliance on maturity as the driver for change will come to an end. Adopting these frameworks, when viewed through the prism of becoming a learning and disciplined organization, will take on a new meaning and focus.

At the same time, you must recognize that simply adopting one or all of these frameworks is not enough. There are countless organizations that have invested decades of resource time and millions of dollars in these efforts and are no closer to becoming a learning and disciplined organization than they were on day one. In the end, becoming a learning and disciplined organization actually has little to do with the organization – it is really all about the individuals who make up your organization. Therefore, you must be prepared to operate at a somewhat philosophical level at times. You must devote significant energy to espousing the concepts and ideas put forth in this chapter. You must spend time talking with your team about what it means to be a learning organization. You must take the time to help them understand what true discipline really means.

This may sound frothy, but the ideas are important. Your people need to understand what this is really about. It is the only way that you can truly focus on enabling personal accountability and responsibility, which are the core foundations for becoming a learning and disciplined organization – and for everything that will follow.

While I cannot cover everything here, there are a few key principles that you should embrace as you begin your journey to becoming a learning and disciplined organization.

Shared, aspirational vision

If there is one thing that is lacking in almost every IT organization I have worked with, it is a clear and compelling aspirational vision. There are sometimes slogans. There is sometimes a 'mission statement.' There is often a strategic plan. But rarely is there a powerful, unifying, aspirational vision that binds the organization together. It's a shame, because I believe that it is the single greatest determinant of whether you will succeed in building a Quantum IT organization.

I remember the day in 1992 when we were first given our new moniker. Our CIO brought together our team and christened us "The Dream Team." I was relatively new in my career and this was my first taste of being part of something big. She laid it out for us. A vision for the adventure that we were about to embark upon. The road was going to be rough, she told us. There would be many sleepless nights. Most people would have no appreciation of the work we were about to do or the true, lasting impact it would have on the organization. But what we were doing was vital to our healthcare organization being competitive, and surviving, and making a difference in the lives of the patients we cared for. Others may not understand or notice how vital our work was to all of this. But she knew. And we would know.

With that send-off, we set out to convert our chain of hospitals from System 36's to a centralized AS/400 platform. The nights were long and the appreciation was scant, but we knew why we were working so hard and what we were achieving at the end of it. When we finished, ahead of schedule and below budget, having amazed the executive staff and hospital administrators with how efficient and painless the process had been, we knew we had succeeded. We had realized our vision.

This is the power of a truly aspirational vision. It inspires us. It makes us want to be a part of something bigger than ourselves. It helps us to see our work in a broader context – to see the value that our work creates. And it inherently creates a mental framework that preconditions us to become accountable, disciplined and open to continuous change and improvement. But there was another factor in this story. This was not just our CIO's vision. She offered it to us. She asked us to make it our own. And we did. We embraced it. She didn't try to own it or control it. She invited us to join her. We had a job to do. But we also had a choice. And by making that choice, we crossed a line and joined "The Dream Team." From that moment on, our personal motivations became secondary. It was all about achieving the vision – together.

For an IT leader, there may be no more powerful or effective tool to building a learning and disciplined organization than creating an aspirational vision. But doing so takes courage. It takes an extraordinary level of faith in your team. It means that you must be willing to let go of much of the control that you've been conditioned to hold onto. It also means that you must be prepared to live up to the vision you've created.

I remember one night during my time on "The Dream Team," I had come in on the weekend because something had to be done. But I had my kids that weekend and had to bring them with me. As I walked into the data center, there was my CIO at a console working away. What would she say about the fact that I'd brought my kids to work? Would I get reprimanded? Told to go home? Instead, she became the CIO-babysitter, taking the kids to the break room and keeping them occupied so that I could keep things moving. The vision of what we were doing transcended roles and positions. We were in this together and we were all going to do whatever was required to realize that vision. Her actions that day made it very clear to all of us.

You must always think of your IT organization as a 'band of brothers' on a journey toward a destination that is constantly changing and evolving. Whether you run the entire organization or are a 'leader of one,' you must always have a vision – a destination in mind. That vision must be bigger than you. It must be something that can transcend the organization and become a shared vision.

Once you've created it, and offered it up as a gift to your team, you will have laid the cornerstone for creating a learning and disciplined organization.

Personal accountability

I have mentioned personal accountability a few times, but it is important to address it here because it is so easy to simply nod agreement and move on. There is a lot of talk about personal accountability in corporate circles today, but frankly not a lot exists. But the lack of personal accountability is the hidden destroyer of value in most IT organizations.

The general lack of personal accountability is responsible for vast amounts of the challenges that face modern IT organizations. The endless cycles of decision-by-consensus, the bureaucratic monstrosities that we create, the endless governance committees – while they are all framed in some other context, fundamentally they are rooted in a general unwillingness of IT professionals at all levels to take personal accountability.

But personal accountability is about more than just taking responsibility for your actions. That is where it starts, of course. But that is actually the easy part. Most people are willing to do that. But the personal accountability that I am talking about here means taking responsibility for an outcome, even when you cannot fully control it. In the Ritz-Carlton example, the accountability is to the performance as a team. Team members feel responsible for the outcome, not just their individual component of it. Therefore, they are empowered to act to make things right – they feel that they have a duty to act.

Whereas a shared vision is best viewed as a gift that you share with others, personal accountability is an expectation – which begins with you. Perhaps ironically, the greatest deterrent to someone's being willing to accept this kind of personal accountability is the belief that no one else will. It feels fruitless and downright foolish to be the chump accepting full responsibility for everything that is going wrong around you, knowing that your peers are snickering in the corner. It is this fear that stops most people from taking the first step forward. But once someone does, it has a dramatic effect. The entire process begins to work in reverse.

At one point in my career, I was given an impossible task. I was told that we needed to take 35 sites that we were acquiring from another company and completely refit them. New PCs, new printers, new terminals, new network cabling, connected to a new WAN, connected to a new data center. All in three months.

I tried to keep it together. I was projecting strength and confidence – or so I thought. But the look on my face must have been priceless. My CIO looked me in the eyes and said, "Don't worry. Do your best. I know you can do this. And I'll take any heat that comes. So you just go out there and do your job."

And she did. The power of that simple statement – and the actions that backed up the words – had a cascading affect. Because she was willing to step up and take responsibility for whatever happened, I was suddenly freed to take greater risks and to operate without fear. That, in turn, created a strong sense of empowerment within me that poured out onto my team. And before I knew it, there I was making the same kind of statement to my team. And so it went. Like a wildly contagious virus, people at all levels of the organization were standing up and taking accountability for things that they had no control over. Because they knew that they were not standing alone.

You cannot mandate personal accountability. You can set up control mechanisms to enforce rules – and you should. But the kind of personal accountability we are talking about here only happens one way – when one person is willing to step out and turn the cycle around. If you are going to be a leader in the Quantum Age, that person is you.

Systems thinking and representative versus representation

Have you ever contemplated how many of the challenges within IT organizations are caused simply by the fact that we operate in silos? That most of the time we fail to look beyond our immediate borders to understand the potential impact of our actions on others? The entire foundation of becoming a learning organization is the concept of systems thinking – of seeing everything as interconnected to other components of the greater system. The challenge with systems thinking is that it's easy to grasp conceptually, but difficult to put into practice. It runs counter to so many of the organizational artifacts that have existed for generations, that the path of least resistance is simply the way things have always been done.

Fully embracing systems thinking requires a discipline and commitment of its own. But every organization can move a long way down this road with a simple change in approach: moving from a representation model to a representative model.

The mood was somber. The outage had been bad. Very bad. It was early in my time with the healthcare company and the impact had been felt throughout the entire organization. And we knew we'd blown it. There I sat at the head of a long table. Each major area of IT operations was represented to try to figure out what had happened and how we could be sure that it would not happen again. Before I could even get the meeting started, it began. The finger-pointing. Every group defending their position and their actions. It's a common scene in IT organizations.

"Let me start this meeting by saying that I accept full blame and responsibility for this outage," I opened the meeting. "Blame is settled and it lies solely with me. Now that the question of blame and responsibility is off the table, I would like to spend the rest of this meeting dissecting what happened so that we can make sure that it does not happen again. To do that, I want everyone to take off your badges. You do not represent your area at this meeting. You are witnesses. Together, we are going to walk through this. We are simply trying to figure out what happened and why, as a team. So that, as a team, we can make sure that it never happens again. That is our sole objective."

After a few moments of stunned silence, one of the network guys spoke up and told the group how he first became aware of the situation. Then it came out in a flood. The story of how this event had unfolded was told by the group in a fluid manner, with one person filling in the holes of someone else until the whole story had emerged. Gone was the posturing. Gone was the defensiveness. Gone were the explanations. The entire mood of the group changed. What started out as negativity turned into excitement as they began to explore ways to improve things as a team.

In truth, it had started as an experiment. I wanted to see if, by handling it differently, I could get a better result. How it turned out surprised even me. While it was an incredibly painful episode, it also turned out to be the single greatest source of improvement for our operational protocols that we had ever had. There were a vast number of changes that came out of that one meeting and they were all embraced by the entire operational team. Not because they were particularly brilliant, but because all of the normal defense mechanisms had been torn down during that initial conversation. Months later, people were still talking about that one meeting and the impact that it had.

As I later reflected on what had happened and the dramatically different result this approach evoked, the one great thing that had changed occurred to me. The approach changed the group of people from representatives – there to represent and defend their team – to a representative group that was there to solve a common problem.

This is a subtle, but extremely important, distinction. When someone views him- or herself as a representative, their primary objective is to protect the interest of those they represent. It is a fundamentally defensive and protective posture. This is what happens most of the time when we attempt to engage cross-functional teams. People come together, seeing themselves representing their team. But when cross-functional teams are being brought together, that is rarely the objective. What we are seeking is to create a representative group. A group that, through the different experiences, perspectives, and insights of its members, can create something that no one group could create on its own. We must be cognizant of this dynamic and fight the natural tendency for cross-functional teams to see themselves as representatives, creating instead representative teams. It is one of the key building blocks of creating a learning organization.

Expose assumptions and challenge mental models

Even if you have gotten this far and created a shared, aspirational vision, created a sense of personal accountability, and begun to truly embrace systems thinking, there are still two hidden landmines that are just waiting to destroy your efforts: assumptions and mental models.

We like to think of ourselves as highly rational people. We do things for reasons that make sense. We do them for the right reasons. I truly believe that most people are good at their core. Most of us do what we think is right, for the right reasons. We are not trying to be mean or stupid or vindictive. There are exceptions, of course, but in my experience this is the truth most of the time.

But when we step away from a situation, oftentimes the actions that we take do not hold up. They do, in fact, seem mean or ill-intentioned. At the least, they often look misinformed, sloppy, arrogant, or sometimes just plain dumb. But why? The reason is that we are often being much less rational than we think. Our subconscious mind is a powerful thing and it can cause us to do things that in retrospect or from an objective perspective make no sense at all.

In his book *Predictably Irrational*, Daniel Ariely lays out example after example of this exact thing. He does a great job of explaining the underlying causes of our seemingly irrational behavior and shows that we are, somewhat ironically, consistent in our irrationality. This is in sharp contrast to the image that most of us have of ourselves and our organizations – that we are perfectly rational and that our organizations operate in an unemotional state. But as Ariely repeatedly shows, this is patently untrue. As humans we are not nearly as rational as we believe ourselves to be and we are predominately driven by emotion. And as organizations are merely large groups of individuals, they too are largely emotionally driven.

Senge picks up this same line of thought when he identifies two of the greatest barriers to creating a learning organization. He points out that we all operate from a set of assumptions and combine those assumptions into sets of 'mental models' which subconsciously guide our actions and perceptions. This is fundamentally the same psychological underpinnings at work that Ariely describes. In order to function, our subconscious creates these sets of assumptions and mental models to enable us to rapidly discern our environment, prioritize, and take action. In the 2011 German documentary *The Automatic Brain*, the producers examine the power of the subconscious. According to their research, conscious thought takes 500 times the energy that subconscious activity does. Therefore, a vast amount of what we do is necessarily handled subconsciously.

This is, of course, a great thing. It is this dynamic use of our subconscious, to handle the everyday, trivial activities, that allows us to function and be productive. Without it, we literally couldn't walk and talk at the same time. Without the power of our subconscious mind enabling us to process the vast amount of 'real-time data' about our environment and what is happening around us, we would be reduced to simpleminded organisms sitting there trying to consciously process every bit of information as it comes to us.

But while our subconscious is vital to our ability to operate and function as humans, it sometimes, as both Ariely and the *Automatic Mind* series demonstrate, works against us. The assumptions and mental models that Senge describes are a case in point. As we gain experience in IT, we begin building these sets of assumptions and mental models. We learn to recognize patterns that enable us to rapidly assess a situation and respond. This is vital to doing our jobs. The problem is that the world of IT is in a state of constant change. And sometimes those changes cause a disruption to those assumptions that we've built up. The world around us has changed, but our assumptions and the mental models that we use to react to that world have not. This happens a lot more than we think or realize.

I remember one particular meeting where this was made very clear to us. The team of middle managers shuffled into the room. Representing teams from across the very large financial organization, they came from two camps: infrastructure and applications. These two groups barely knew each other. Many of them were meeting for this first time in that very room. We had been told about some of the challenges, so we actually arranged seating in a boy-girl-boy-girl fashion, with an infrastructure person sitting next to an apps person sitting next to an infrastructure person, and so on.

As the meeting wore on, the most valuable moments were when 'clashes of clarity' would break out somewhere around the table. Someone would say something and the person sitting next to him would say something to the effect of, "Oh yeah? You think that's what happened? Let me tell you what happened when it got to me." And a dialogue would take place. The first person would end up saying something like, "Really? I had no idea that it had that impact."

We covered a lot of ground during that two-day workshop. But unquestionably, the greatest thing that came out of the meeting was that people began to challenge their assumptions of how things worked, of what expectations others had of their services, of the impact that their actions had on others. It is in such cases that the power of assumptions and mental models works against us. Because they are designed to operate 'under the surface,' we are rarely aware that they even exist. They guide our actions, our thought processes, and our perspectives, but they do it in many cases without our ever realizing it. And that means that we will rarely challenge them or adapt them as our environment changes. I have no doubt whatsoever that I harbor a set of assumptions and mental models that are rooted in my first few years in the business over 20 years ago. You do too. But do you believe for a minute that they are still valid?

The fact that these assumptions and mental models lie beneath the surface makes them hard to address. The first step is simply to recognize them. By acknowledging that much of what we do is based upon these assumptions and mental models, we will be giving ourselves the authority to see them and challenge them. It is also important to note that this must begin with the challenging of your own assumptions. You cannot point out someone else's assumptions and mental models as a means of creating a learning organization. You can only unabashedly expose your own assumptions and ask others to do the same. It requires a level of both humility and vulnerability, but it will be the watershed moment for your team.

The next time you are in a meeting, try this. Begin the meeting by stating your belief, but then explore and expose the assumptions that are guiding your decision and invite others to engage you on the veracity of your assumptions. It might go something like this:

I have called this meeting because we need to deal with an important situation. We simply have too many critical incidents in our environment and I have been tasked with resolving this situation and finding some solution immediately. I believe that we need to immediately appoint a critical-incident leader who will always be on call and will be personally accountable for the resolution of a critical incident.

This is where a conversation like this typically stops. The group will then begin discussing how to make this happen, how to deal with the logistics, when they should be called, and so on. But what would happen if you then added one more thing?

Now, before we dive in to make this happen, I want to tell you why I believe this. It is based on a set of assumptions that I am making. So the first step is to validate that these assumptions are correct, because if they're not, then we're probably barking up the wrong tree here. I believe that the single greatest problem we have is that when there is a major incident, there is no one person accountable for resolving the situation. Everyone scrambles to try to help, but because no one owns it, decisions don't get made or they take too long. And because no one person is in charge, there is also no single point of communication out to our affected customers. That's why I think that this is the proper course of action. But my assumptions may be wrong. Tell me if you believe that they are correct or not.

Suddenly, this moves from a conversation about you and your ideas to a conversation about an underlying set of assumptions. It will completely change the dynamic of the meeting. It will cause everyone in the meeting to expose their assumptions and lead to a true dialogue. Through that dialogue, true learning will occur. It may turn out that the course of action was correct. But even if that is the case, it will now be rooted in a solid base of understanding as to why it is the correct course of action.

Practice, practice, practice

When we first decided to take tennis lessons, we started with a group lesson. One of the people in our group was this great gal named Katie. She was just a lot of fun. She had a sharp wit and a dry sense of humor and she just made the lessons fun – and somewhat unpredictable. At one point, our tennis coach John was giving her some instruction. He was walking her through a motion and he said, "Whenever you are practicing, just imagine that I am there with you." To which she replied, "John, every time I am practicing, you are with me!"

Like many of us, she did not practice. For most of us, practicing is not something that we consider enjoyable. Or, for that matter, a good use of time. It feels like a waste. "I don't have time to practice, I have too much real work to do." Unfortunately, most of us learn most easily by doing something. Reading about it does not do it. Hearing about it does not do it. Watching someone does not do it. Most of the time, we have to do something before we'll even begin to truly learn it. This is why it is often said that the best way to learn something is to teach it to someone else. It sounds counterintuitive, but teaching it involves a form of simply doing it, so it forces us to internalize it.

For most things in life, this process happens naturally. 'On-the-job training' has been the way that most of us have learned almost everything we know. There is nothing wrong with this. It works. The challenge when it comes to applying these key principles of the learning and disciplined organization is that because many of these principles are not actively practiced in day-to-day operations, there is no place, no way, to learn them 'on the job.' As your organization matures, that will change. But, in the beginning, you need to create opportunities to practice these techniques so that they can develop into a discipline in their own right.

While this can seem to be one of those 'soft exercises,' an interesting thing happens. Because you are fundamentally learning skills and ways of interacting, these practice sessions begin to lead to real-world results in ways that were not intended or anticipated. So don't fool yourself. The practice we are talking about here is real and will manifest itself in tangible ways.

So what does it mean to create 'practice opportunities'? Mostly, it means giving people the time to experiment with these concepts and put them into practice. It will be most effective if this is done in the context of real, but perhaps not critical, business problems. Create a team to solve some long-standing and nagging problem. But do not allow them to immediately start building a solution as IT folks often do. Start by asking them to create an aspirational vision that frames what the solution to the problem will *feel* like when it is realized. How can the answer to this simple, perhaps inconsequential, problem be used as an aspirational goal?

Then ask them to self-organize and create their own charter. Do not give them anything more than the problem as guidance. Make them personally accountable for the success and execution of the effort – as a team – from start to finish. Challenge their functional allegiances, within the context of the team, and make them responsible for areas that are far outside the bounds of their normal functional responsibilities. Ask them to begin every meeting by stating their idea or position and then exposing their assumptions and inviting others to challenge them.

Creating practice fields of these kinds will have a dramatic impact on your teams. It will teach them to look at problems differently. It will create new connections and relationships amongst your team members. It will forever alter long-held perceptions. And it will lay the foundation for creating a true learning and disciplined organization.

It may feel like this is a wasted exercise. The squandering of highly paid, valuable resources. But after only a short period of time you will see things start to change. By giving your teams the opportunity to practice this approach, it will begin to change how they approach problems in their everyday work life. It will begin to become second nature for them to ask to understand the vision, to instill accountability within their teams, and to expose assumptions. They will begin, perhaps unknowingly, to embed these principles into their day-to-day activities. At that point, the traditional 'on-the-job' training approach will begin to take root and the core principles of becoming a learning and disciplined organization will begin to become infused into the fabric of your culture.

Chapter 7 key points

Becoming a learning and disciplined organization is a never-ending journey. It involves the adoption of frameworks such as ITIL and CMMi, but it's really about the individuals that make up your organization. You must invest in them and in ensuring that they have the tools that they need to take your organization into the future.

Here are the key points you should remember from this chapter:

- A powerful, unifying, aspirational vision that binds the organization together may be the single greatest determinant of success in building a Quantum IT organization.

- A vision is a destination – a place you want to reach in the future. It must be bigger than you and it must be something that can transcend and unify the organization.

- The lack of personal accountability is the hidden destroyer-of-value in most IT organizations.

- Personal accountability must go beyond simply being responsible for your own actions, you must be accountable for the team's outcomes and performance – not just your piece of it.

- The key to becoming a learning organization is the embrace of systems thinking. The easiest first step is to move your organization from a representations model (where people represent their respective silo or function) to a representative model (where people come together to represent the organization as a whole).

- The two hidden land mines that are waiting to destroy your efforts are assumptions and mental models.

- You must create practice opportunities to give people the time to experiment and put ideas into practice.

CHAPTER 8: TEARING DOWN THE WALL: CREATING A TRANSPARENT AND INTIMATE ORGANIZATION

Bill Wray is not an IT person. But he was a great CIO.

Beginning his career in civil engineering, he was never really content to define himself by what he did. He preferred to define himself by how he did it. "I have always been a restless problem solver," is how he puts it. His mantra is simple. He always asks a simple question: "Can we make it better?"

After deciding that he did not care for civil engineering, he moved first into real estate and then banking. He found himself at Citizen's Bank during the mad rush of Y2K and was given an opportunity – a challenge, really. Could he make it better? He took the challenge, despite knowing almost nothing about IT. Eventually, he rose to the rank of CIO and led a series of massive integration efforts. That led to a new opportunity as CIO for Blue Cross Blue Shield of Rhode Island, where he has now been promoted to the role of COO.

Throughout his career, Wray took what many surely saw as a negative and turned it into a positive. His lack of technology skills and history was undoubtedly met with skepticism and doubt by his team when he first joined the ranks of IT professionals. After all, how could he contribute to a technology department without knowing anything about technology? But this also offered him a unique perspective. He did not look at IT as technology. He saw it as a tool to solve problems. And solving problems was his business, his skill.

His lack of a technology background also offered him another distinct advantage: he had nothing to protect. He was not married to technology. It was not his identity. With his identity based solidly in the role of problem solver, nothing was sacred. And that meant that he could be as open and as transparent as he wanted to be with his customers. At the same time, because he began his career (and would subsequently continue it) outside IT, he had a built-in ability to relate to his customers on their turf. He spoke their language and they could sense that he was 'on their side.' As a result, he had an IT career that had a significant, positive impact on his customers – and he created IT organizations that were engaged and, frankly, had a lot of fun.

Through a combination of circumstance and attitude, Wray created and led IT organizations that delivered on the true promise of IT. They were engaged with their customers, relentlessly driven to deliver, and empowered to understand what that truly meant in the language of their customers. That is good IT. That is good business. And it is the type of IT organization that serves as a model for building the transparent and intimate IT organizations of the Quantum Age.

Come look under the hood

When we moved to Newport Beach, California, one of the first, most important tasks was to find a good mechanic. In California, there is no 'tool' more important to daily survival than our cars. Having a good, reliable, and affordable mechanic is an absolute requirement. But they can be hard to find.

8: Tearing down the Wall

Luckily for me, I found Marcus. Marcus is not your typical mechanic. In fact, I am not even sure that he knows how to fix a car. I have never seen him work on one. But what he does do is build a relationship with his customers.

It is a relationship based on two simple things: trust and choice.

Whenever I take my car into Marcus, I know, through experience, what I will get. First, he is simply going to ask me what is wrong. He is not going to try to give me an immediate solution or some preset answer. He is simply going to listen and then say, "OK, let me take a look and I'll tell you what I find."

Second, I know that he is going to tell me the reality of the situation straight. No opaqueness. No hiding behind technical jargon and mumbo jumbo. He is simply going to give me the straight scoop on what is up with my car. And sometimes, that means that he is going to tell me that he does not know for sure and that the best he can do is give me his best guess as to what is happening.

Finally, I know that I am going to get some options. Given the situation, he is going to tell me how I can respond to it and how much each of those responses will cost. He will give me the relative pros and cons of each option, including the potential risk (if any) with any given option. And one of the options will ALWAYS be to do nothing – delivered with a clear understanding of the potential risk or impact of doing nothing.

When I was young, I used to work on my own car. But that was back in the day when cars still had carburetors. Today, when I open the hood, I have almost no idea what I am looking at. And Marcus never asks me to. He simply explains the situation, and my options, in terms that I can understand. So that I can make the right decision for me. This is what transparency is all about.

But when we talk about transparency in IT circles, that is not what we are normally meaning. If IT organizations are even using the term 'transparency,' they normally mean the opposite of the approach that Marcus takes. We open up the hood, point to the spaghetti of wires and valves and say, "See what I mean. It's a mess. Just look at the <insert some technical mumbo jumbo here> ... and that is why you need to approve my request."

That is our idea of transparency. No choice. No understanding of the situation in simple, business terms. Just a hope and a prayer that if we can keep them confused enough, they will just give us the approval that we want.

I know that this sounds harsh. And I truly believe that most IT professionals are not doing this because they're trying to get something over on anyone. We generally believe that the solution that we are proposing is the right one. But this is the reality of how transparency is often treated by IT – and it must stop.

What are we afraid of?

There is a reason why we do this. Fear. We are afraid that the customer will 'make the wrong decision.' What we really want is for them to trust us. We believe that they are paying us for our expertise and that they should therefore trust our recommendations when we make them. If we are being honest with ourselves, we are actually a little put off by the fact that we have to justify our recommendation at all. We believe that it is a clear sign that they have no faith in us and feel that they must check and validate everything we do.

Sound about right?

But let me ask you a question. Do you believe that because Marcus gives me the situation straight, because he offers me choices and tells me the pros, cons, and risks of each, it causes me to respect him less? That it means that I do not trust him? Absolutely not. In fact, I would argue, it has the exact opposite effect. Because he treats me with respect, because he speaks to me in my terms, the first question I almost always ask is, "OK, thanks. So, what do you recommend?" Nine times out of ten, I take his recommendation. His transparent approach instills a deep sense of trust and faith. It communicates that he has nothing to hide and that he respects that, in the end, I am the one who is purchasing and receiving the service. Therefore, I am the only one ultimately capable of determining the best choice for me.

This is the divide that we must cross as IT organizations and as IT professionals. We must come to the relationship with our customer with humility and an attitude that we are there to serve them. We must have confidence in our abilities and with the due diligence that we provide that we can go into the relationship with nothing to hide. As we do, we will begin to change and shape the relationship with our customers.

Transparency = choice

Perhaps the most difficult thing for IT professionals to fully grasp is that transparency is not really about 'spilling our guts.' It is solely about choice. It is about giving our customer enough information, which includes our assessment, opinions, and recommendations, to enable them to make the best decisions possible. But that level of information is almost never technical in nature. As the saying goes, the customer does not really want to see 'how the sausage is made.'

We are fearful of sharing too much information with the customer because we believe that they cannot understand it. We do not want to give them a choice because we fear that if they do not understand the information that we have shared with them, then they will make the wrong choice. But this is not a reflection on the customer or the process. It is a reflection on the information that we are providing to them. If the customer cannot understand the situation to a point where they can make a good decision, then that means that we are not giving them the right kind of information. We are giving them technical information when what they need is business information.

Premier is one of the largest providers of healthcare data in the country. That puts them in the center of a rapidly changing industry with intense data needs. Joe Pleasant, CIO of Premier, has made a commitment to making transparency a core quality within the organization. Each year, they take their core service offerings to their internal customers and, in effect, perform their own competitive analysis. They tell them what has changed in the marketplace since the last review and present them with all the options available – specifically those that are available from outside the IT organization. Sounds crazy, doesn't it? Going to your customer and making sure they know about all of your competition?

But Pleasant sees it differently. "Who is better suited to help them evaluate their options than IT?" he says. "Because we do this, it generates a tremendous amount of trust in us. Sometimes, we have to be willing to tell them that someone else can do something better than we can, but that normally means that it is the right decision for the company."

This attitude and approach has enabled Pleasant and his IT organization to thrive and to adapt in a very tumultuous time in the healthcare industry. He feels that it helps to keep them on their toes. They know that they are going to subject themselves to competitive scrutiny, every year. So they rally around to ensure not only that they are doing things right, but that they are doing the right things. It creates an incentive for the team to recognize the services that are not within their core capabilities and the freedom to let those services go to someone who is going to do a better job for the company. It takes courage. It takes faith in your ability to deliver what you promise you will deliver. And it takes the wisdom and honesty to recognize those things that you will not be able to deliver as well as someone else.

But it also takes one more thing: the right kind of information. One of Pleasant's rules is that the service and market analysis that they perform is strictly in business terms. No technology jargon allowed. They speak in terms of capabilities, results and outcomes. Not technology. It is a discipline that they have built and honed over time. It puts the power of choice into the hands of their customers. And elevates them as the trusted partner and provider of choice because of it.

This is what it means to be a transparent organization. It is one that does not hide behind technology. It is one that comes to the customer on their terms, speaking their language. One that comes bearing choices and the analysis of those choices to help the customer make the right and best decision. And one that, in the end, shows respect for the customer as the sole arbiter of value.

Crossing the intimacy line

Mojgan Lefebvre has a routine. She has enjoyed a rapid rise as a senior IT executive. This has involved a number of new positions as she has taken on greater and greater challenges. And each time, she starts at the same place. Talking with her customers.

She sets up meetings with each of them with a simple, single aim: to quickly understand what they care about. She does not start by telling them everything she is going to do. She does not trot out her seven-point improvement plan. She starts by listening. She comes to their turf, speaks their language, and simply seeks to understand. Once she does, she works with them to come up with two or three indicators that reflect what they care about. And that is how she begins her relationship with them.

Now the CIO of Liberty Mutual's Commercial Markets Division, this routine has served her well. It has the immediate effect of changing the dynamic and often contentious relations that she is stepping into. By coming to them seeking to understand, she is visibly communicating that the focus is on them as her customer. And the impact on the relationship and what she is then able to get accomplished is one of the secrets to her string of successes and rapid rise in the executive ranks.

Bill Wray of Blue Cross Blue Shield of Rhode Island calls this the 'intimacy line.' "I tell my team that we cannot be satisfied meeting our customer 'in the middle.' 50% of the way is not good enough. We need to go 80% of the way and let them come the last 20% to us. We need to go where they work and take the middlemen out of our relationship with our customer," he says.

Not expecting your customer to meet you in the middle. Going into the relationship with a belief that you must go 80% of the way to create the kind of relationship you need. Is that what it takes? What does it mean to become 'intimate' with our customer? Is that what we are really supposed to do?

Intimacy is a bit of a strange word in the business environment. Michael Treacy and Fred Wiersema first introduced the concept of 'customer intimacy' in a 1993 *Harvard Business Review* article. They defined customer intimacy as combining "detailed customer knowledge with operational flexibility so they can respond quickly to almost any need." While the concept has been circulating for decades in marketing circles, it is still not a word that is thrown around much within IT. From an IT perspective, it means establishing a robust relationship with your customer that goes far beyond 'getting requirements' and 'delivering to the SLA.' It means that through the process of creating and maintaining deep relationships with your customers, you cease being 'the IT person' and simply become viewed as an extension of their team. The intimacy line that Wray spoke of is really a way of saying that you need to put yourself in their shoes, communicate in their terms and focus on how they produce value ... and then explore how IT can help support that process.

Ashwin Rangan, the current CIO at Edwards Lifesciences, has served in senior executive roles at Walmart, Bank of America and Conexant Systems. He says that his secret starting point whenever he finds himself in a new role is to go and talk to the Chief Marketing Officer. "Whenever I start at a new organization, one of the first people that I go to see is the CMO. Remarkably, I am almost always the first IT executive that has come to their office, sat down, and simply talked about what they are doing and how I can help," he says. But it is one of the most important meetings he has, Rangan continues, because it connects him to the core of what the business is really doing from a customer and marketing perspective – and that gives him a foundation from which to understand how IT can best support and extend the value from those efforts.

In each of these cases, Lefebvre, Wray, and Rangan all begin the process of enabling IT to deliver rapid and meaningful value through the simple process of listening. Rangan actually compares the process to that of courting a future spouse. "When you met your future spouse, you did not immediately propose," he says. "You began with a simple date. You got to know them and let them get to know you. You shared your dreams, aspirations and history. And most importantly, you just spent time together. A business relationship really isn't very different."

But it is this view of an intimate relationship between IT and its customers that can scare some people. There is no option to have an arm's length relationship when you go down this road. And just like a marriage, as the relationship progresses and matures, expectations are raised. In short, creating an intimate relationship means becoming vulnerable.

The courage to be vulnerable

Accepting the idea of being vulnerable, particularly in a business setting, can be tough for some people according to Rangan. "When you're in an intimate relationship at the personal level, you agree to be in a mutually vulnerable relationship. That's a mind bender for a lot of people. The mutual vulnerability defies definition. You have to be willing to let it all hang out," he explains.

But while that can seem scary, vulnerability is the exact opposite of what we encounter in most business situations: protective walls, defensiveness, keeping your head down. In fact, it is the complete lack of intimacy that causes the vast majority of miscommunication, in-fighting, and generally destructive behavior in organizations. That is because while establishing an intimate relationship involves mutual vulnerability, that vulnerability is only accepted if it is founded on a relationship of trust. The trust that underpins an intimate relationship is the game-changer.

Have you ever noticed the difference between a healthy relationship and an unhealthy one? Some people think it is that there is less fighting in a healthy relationship. But that really is not true. The difference is that in a healthy relationship, there is a foundation of trust that lets both people know that they are on safe ground. The foundation of their relationship is in bedrock and will not be rocked by any minor disagreement. So they are free to express what they are really feeling; as Rangan says, "to let it all hang out." The fight might get loud and angry and messy, but in the end they know that it will get resolved somehow, some way, and everything will be fine. It is that bedrock foundation of trust and what it says about the relationship that lets a disagreement play out in a way that actually produces a resolution. And then they can move on, with their relationship actually stronger from the process.

It is a fun bit of irony that it is actually their willingness to be mutually vulnerable that makes their relationship less vulnerable.

We must seek the same kind of trust-driven, built-on-bedrock relationships with our customers. It is only through this type of intimate relationship that we are freed to do the two things that are required to fundamentally transform IT into the organization that it must become: *tell the truth* and *discover the truth*.

Tell the truth. Discover the truth.

The dirty little secret in IT organizations is that we are often afraid to tell our customer the truth. We are sure that they will not understand. Or that they will not believe us. Or that they simply will not care. In either case, we are sure that if we do not tell them what they want to hear, they will pull our funding or otherwise make our life miserable. So, we make promises that we cannot possibly keep. We put together complex ROIs that are all but made up. We have this deep-seated desire to tell our customer the words made famous by Jack Nicholson in the movie *A Few Good Men*: "You can't handle the truth!"

But it is the truth that they need to hear. And, contrary to what we may believe, they want to hear it. What they do not want is to get what they believe to be an arbitrary 'no.' They want options and they want the straight story. But it is often the lack of a truly intimate relationship that stops us from being willing to give it to them. But, like the couple above, if an intimate relationship exists, we become freed to speak plainly about the situation and even have a 'spirited conversation' about it because we know that our relationship is built upon a bedrock foundation of trust. The power of the intimate relationship is that it allows us to be fully candid with our customers, to tell them what they need to hear and to be prepared to hear what they have to say.

The freedom of telling the truth lays the foundation for honest dialogue. We become less concerned with 'saying the right thing' or not stirring up a political hornets' nest because we have faith that our relationship is strong enough to withstand any fallout. Through the dialogue that results, we are able to get to the heart of the matter. And, like the healthy couple, we are able to bring the issue to resolution, true resolution.

But the intimacy of the relationship allows us to go beyond just telling the truth. It allows us to discover the truth. Or, perhaps more accurately, it allows us to simply know the truth most of the time and discover the truth when we do not already know it.

If you have ever been in a serious, personal relationship you probably know what I mean. When you are in that type of a relationship, the intimacy between the two of you transcends virtually every facet of your life. Simply based on the nature of your relationship, you can probably tell me vast amounts of information about what your significant other likes or does not like. About what gets them going and fired up and what will cause them to disengage. You will instinctively know when they are going to like how a situation plays out and that it will make them happy, or if you are going to be in for a rough night. It is not that at any point they tell you all of these things. It is simply through the closeness of the relationship, through the history of shared experiences, that you develop an innate knowledge of how they think, how they react and what they want and need out of life.

Of course, if you have been in a serious relationship, you also know that this is not always the case.

Sometimes what they do makes no sense to you at all. Sometimes you sit there, just scratching your head, baffled. Their actions or reactions do not seem to line up at all with what you expected. No matter how close the relationship, this always happens at some point. We are human. We are not machines. How we will act or react cannot always be predicted – in some case, even by ourselves. But even in these cases, the intimacy of our relationship provides a safety valve. It gives us the means to discover this previously unknown truth. It gives us a platform from which we can seek to understand what is going on and continue to build our relationship and our knowledge of each other.

It is the exact same thing with our customers. When we move beyond a relationship built on 'requirements' and 'delivering against SLAs,' when we build a truly intimate relationship with our customer, it starts looking a lot more like the description above. You will simply stop asking them the exacting detail of their every need and you will instead simply know it. You will bring them solutions to problems that they either did not know existed or never thought to ask about – and they will be delighted by this newly discovered option. And, occasionally, there will be a situation in which things do not line up. But, just like in our personal relationships, having this level of intimacy will give us the platform from which to discover the truth. You will come to them with a genuine desire to understand.

Gone will be the days of, 'Just tell me what you want!' and they will be replaced with, 'Hmmm. I really thought I understood. I thought that this would be something that would help your situation. I obviously missed something somewhere. Can you help me understand what is really going on so that I can see how I can help?'

That is a fundamentally different conversation, but that is because it is based on a fundamentally different relationship. When your relationship with your customer becomes truly intimate, it ceases to be transactional and instead becomes a continuum. You both see yourselves as 'in it together,' and you make a continuous series of investments in one another. You each have 'skin in the game' and a vested interest in each other's success. You will have developed a deep knowledge of each other and because of this you will simply treat each other differently. Just as in a personally intimate relationship, above all else you will develop a deep level of comfort with one another and that will allow you to explore new areas together and will open up possibilities that simply cannot be developed any other way. When it works, it is a wondrous thing.

Humility, vulnerability and time

But how do you create this kind of intimate relationship?

It really is not that very different to any other kind of intimate relationship you may have. There are really three key ingredients: humility, vulnerability, and time.

Fair warning: this might hurt a little bit.

I believe that one of the greatest barriers that IT professionals face in building an intimate relationship is a general lack of humility. While we may never be willing to admit it publicly, we have a bit of a superiority complex when it comes to our customers – or, as we more often refer to them, 'the users.' Their stupidity and arrogance never fails to amaze us. It seems to know no end. After all, it is just technology. How can they find it so confusing? Don't they use it every day? How can they keep asking the same silly questions or keep making the same unreasonable requests day after day, month after month, year after year? Don't they ever learn?

Sorry to throw this in your face. But you know it's true. We've all done it. I've done it. I'm not really sure of the reason. Maybe it's to cover up our own insecurity about our lack of knowledge in other areas. Maybe it's simply that technology is our sole worldview and we honestly cannot understand how someone else cannot have the same understanding. But whatever the reason, it causes us to go into relationships with an attitude. Even if we try to 'talk nice,' it seeps out. Whether we're providing support or defining requirements for a new piece of technology or application, they can feel it exuding from our every pore, this sense of exasperation that we even need to be there at all.

And so, they respond in kind. They keep their distance. They see IT as medicine that they know they need to take, but they're going to try to simply get it over with as fast as possible. They don't invest in the relationship. They merely seek to survive it.

It all begins with our lack of humility.

What would happen if we came into the relationship viewing ourselves as a humble servant? Not in the sense of someone subservient to the other person. But rather as someone who had the skills and abilities to help them achieve something that they could not achieve on their own. What if we came to the relationship with an attitude that we were there to serve them, to leverage our unique skills and abilities to help them achieve something great – something that might not be possible without us? And if we saw it as our honor and our privilege to help them achieve it, how might that change the foundation of our relationship?

Of course, that type of approach is scary. That is why you must have the courage to be vulnerable. Humility is the prerequisite for vulnerability. You cannot be vulnerable unless you are first willing to humble yourself. And your willingness to be humble will create a natural vulnerability. But vulnerability is a funny thing. While it requires us to be willing to be insecure and open, it has a powerful affect on the other person. For most people, when they see someone in a vulnerable state, the last thing they want to do is take advantage of it. Instead, it causes a softening. It causes them to become more open. More willing to become vulnerable themselves. And that is the opening that you need to create this kind of truly intimate relationship with your customer.

Once that door is open, only one more thing is required: time.

Intimacy happens in its own time. It cannot be planned. It cannot be rushed. It cannot be scheduled. Perhaps the greatest vulnerability is the fact that you must be willing not to try to control the relationship. You cannot go into it with an 'agenda.' You cannot go into it with a strategy of what you will get out of it. It must be genuine. You must be willing to go into the relationship seeking only to serve. And be willing to continue to invest in the relationship as long as it takes for the relationship to develop.

More than anything else, that means simply spending time together. Spending time simply getting to know each other on a personal level. It means taking the time simply seeking to understand your customers' business, their ambitions, their hopes and dreams – and their fears. It also means that you must begin by seeking to understand for the sake of understanding. Not so that you can dazzle them with a brilliant solution that you whip out of your back pocket. You must simply begin the relationship seeking genuinely to learn about them.

If you think back to when you were still on the 'dating scene,' you'll know what I mean. What were the very worst dates? The ones where the other person spent the entire night talking about themselves, making it very clear that they didn't care about you at all. Or, perhaps even worse, when they spent the entire night trying to fix you. On the other hand, what were the best? It was when the other person came to that first date simply interested in you. They showed genuine interest in your life, your hopes, your plans. That was someone that you wanted to spend more time with, right?

Intimacy comes from this combination of coming to the relationship from a position of humility, being willing to be vulnerable within the relationship and being prepared to invest the time that it takes to let a relationship develop. It might seem strange to think of our relationship with our customers in this way – like we were dating and marrying them. But if you think about it, that is exactly what we're doing. In the end, we are all human. The fundamental emotional and psychological underpinnings drive us in all aspects of our lives. We will always be drawn to work with someone when there is a degree of intimacy involved.

8: Tearing down the Wall

As one last 'proof point' to convince you that you need to understand and learn how to build intimacy with your customers, let me give you one last example. It is tempting to believe that all of this 'intimacy stuff' does not apply to us. The technology services that we are providing are not emotional. They are merely practical. It's just business. So let me pose a scenario. Imagine that you are going to buy a washing machine. Perhaps the epitome of a practical, unsexy piece of technology. You go to the first store. The salesman that greets you asks you for your 'requirements' and based on those facts brings you to a square, white box and says, "Here you go. This one will meet all of your requirements. Will you be taking this with you or do you need it delivered?"

At another store, it's a different approach. The salesman greets you and begins asking you questions about you, your life, and your lifestyle. He seems genuinely interested in you as a person. He tells you a few stories about his own life that are related to yours in some way. He brings you over to a group of washing machines and begins to explain your options. He relates those options to the stories that you've shared. He digresses and tells you a little story about the time his brother had a big accident and how they used a washing machine very similar to the ones you're looking at to 'save the day.' And he ends with, "Now, you shouldn't rush into anything. This can be a big decision. You need to do what is right for you. I am here to help you in any way that I can and if nothing here seems to do the trick, I will be happy to help you find another store that might be able to do a better job for you. Please tell me how I can be of service to you."

This is a washing machine that we're talking about. One of these organizations reduces it to a mere transaction. You will make your decision based solely on price and 'requirements.' Nothing more. With the other organization, in a few short minutes you will feel that you've established some form of genuine relationship. You will feel that they are genuinely looking out for your best interest. And when you make your decision, you will feel good about it – that you had someone on your side helping you make it.

That is customer intimacy. And it is the difference between merely being a service provider and being in a meaningful relationship with your customer.

We are talking about you (yes, really)

There is a chance that you're sitting there, smug in your chair, chuckling. You're thinking, "Boy, my boss is going to have a rough go having to do all of this intimacy stuff."

It is tempting to think that it is always someone else's job to worry about the customer. Especially if you view yourself as primarily a technical person. "They pay me for my technical expertise. I am not a sales or marketing person," you may be muttering to yourself.

It is not uncommon.

We IT people generally enter the field because we are better with technology than we are with people. It is not at all unusual for us to see anything that is not purely technical as just a distraction and a waste of a highly valuable resource – us! At one point in our history, that might have been true. But the world has changed and it is not true any longer. Bill Wray of Blue Cross Blue Shield of Rhode Island says, "The job is not even 80% people anymore. It is 98% about people. IT people have not been able to or wanted to understand that."

8: Tearing down the Wall

No matter what your role in the IT organization – whether you're the CIO, a middle manager, an application developer, a DBA, a network engineer, or a service desk agent – everything that you just read applies to you. You have customers. The services you provide are consumed – either directly or in an aggregate form – by the customer. That means that you must develop the traits of transparency and intimacy in everything you do. You must begin to see everything from the perspective of the customer. You must focus on putting yourself in their shoes, speak their language, and offer them the options that they need to make the business decision possible. You must be willing to go to them, regardless of where you are, and approach them with humility, be willing to be vulnerable and invest the time to really know them.

If you're the CIO, you will be doing this at the most senior and most strategic levels. If you're a network engineer, you will be doing it with your internal customers and, in partnership with them, with those who consume the services you provide. No one is immune. Everyone in the IT organization must understand that these two traits of transparency and intimacy must become embedded at each and every level. This is not the job of some special group somewhere. This is everyone's job. Period.

The idea of creating genuine transparency and building deep, intimate relationships with your customers may seem far-fetched. It is certainly not the norm in the world of IT today. It probably doesn't feel particularly natural. But these are the traits that, built upon the foundation of a learning and disciplined organization, will power the fundamental shift in the relationship between IT and its customers.

That means that it is the most important job that you and everyone else within the IT organization has to do. Will you be courageous? Will you step forward without fear? Will you approach your relationship with your customer with humility and mutual vulnerability? Will you invest the time?

Your customers are genuinely hoping that you will. They are just waiting for you to build the IT organization that you both have always wanted. Transparency and intimacy are the traits you need to get there.

Chapter 8 key points

Beyond learning and discipline are the traits that begin creating a true relationship with your customer: transparency and intimacy. Embracing these traits will move your organization toward delivering on the true promise of IT.

Here are the key points you should remember from this chapter:

- True transparency is not about throwing everything out there to show the complexity of IT so that we can get what we want. True transparency is about choice and options.
- The thing that holds us back from being transparent is fear. We want trust, but it is the fact that we are not fully transparent that hinders true trust between us and our customers.
- By definition, transparency must exist on the customer's terms – we must communicate in the language of business, not technology, in order to be transparent.

- Intimacy starts with listening.
- Intimacy is not about meeting the customer halfway. It is about crossing the 'intimacy line,' going 80% of the way toward your customer.
- Creating customer intimacy is difficult because it requires mutual vulnerability.
- At its core, an intimate relationship with your customer is one built on a bedrock of trust.
- In order to create this type of intimate relationship, there are three key ingredients: humility, vulnerability, and time.

CHAPTER 9: THE IT ORGANIZATION YOUR CUSTOMER ALWAYS WANTED: CREATING THE DYNAMIC ORGANIZATION

When I bought my house in 2001, it came with one additional item that was not listed anywhere on the escrow papers. His name was Felix.

Felix was the gardener who was taking care of the house before we bought it. One morning shortly after we moved in, there was a knock on the door. Felix introduced himself and explained that he'd been taking care of our yard for several years and wanted to know if we wanted him to continue. Truth be told, I had not really given it much thought. Being a California home, it did not have much of a yard to begin with. But still, it had seemed quite beautiful when we bought it, so I figured it made sense to maintain the status quo. It was a good call.

As a man (all stereotypes intended), I am ashamed to admit that I have no desire and almost no knowledge or skills when it comes to all things mechanical – yard work included. Some of my neighbors at the time loved nothing more than to wake up on Saturday morning and spend hours puttering in their yard. For many, it was a sense of pride. It provided a means of tangible accomplishment in a world in which so much of what we do seems so intangible. But for me, it was none of those things. Yard work was (and is) just something that I've always dreaded.

So it was with great relief that I found Felix at my door that morning. It would have been one thing to try to tell my wife that I really didn't want to do the yard work and that I should hire someone. But Felix was already taking care of our yard. I could not, in clear conscience, take away his livelihood after all, could I? And thus began my relationship with Felix. I saved him from having to find a new client – and he saved me from myself.

It did not take Felix very long to find out how much I knew about plants, lawns, sprinklers, outdoor electrical, water lines, and all of that other stuff that is outside the house. When there's nothing there, it doesn't take much. Used to dealing with more 'normal' men, the first time we had to interact he began going into all of the detail about what was going on. He must have noticed the blank stare on my face, because he quickly reduced the level of detail. He stopped talking about the technical aspects of the situation and simply told me the problem, the potential risk or impact, and the options, and asked what I wanted him to do. It was perfect.

Over time, a deep trust developed. I took his advice in almost all ways. Eventually, he got comfortable enough that he began anticipating what I would want and would show up with some equipment and ask if I wanted him to proceed. I almost always did. Along the way, he came to understand what I wanted out of my yard. I wanted it to look neat, tidy, and attractive. But I wanted it to be low-maintenance and low-fuss – except for the fountain that my wife wanted to put in on the side yard. That needed to be special. So that is what we got. A neat, attractive, and simple landscape with an amazing stone waterfall and small stream surrounded by a tropical oasis.

This is not to say that everything always worked. From time to time there would be a problem. Something would break after it had been installed. Or something would cost a lot more than was estimated. But through it all, Felix operated with integrity and made me feel, without a doubt or question, that he was on my side. There was nothing self-serving in anything he did. He knew what I wanted and expected and wanted the same thing for me. He was my 'landscape partner!'

That last bit is a little bit tongue-in-cheek, but the sentiment is real. I loved having Felix around. I knew that I could count on him. I knew that he understood me. He was not going to bore me with technical stuff that I didn't care about. Nor was he going to try to put something over on me. It was a great feeling. I was free simply to enjoy my yard without having to worry about it. While I certainly never referred to him as my 'landscape partner,' in truth that is a lot what it felt like.

This type of relationship, this type of interaction, is what our customers are looking for in their relationship with their IT partners. It really isn't that much to expect and it is not that hard to deliver if we're willing to let go of some of the ties that have bound us to our past. If we are willing to accept new roles and new approaches, this is our future.

Miracles not required

What does your customer really want? This has probably been the question that has plagued IT professionals longer than any other. I don't know if it is that we are wired differently. Or if it's just that we live too close to the technology to be able to see things from the other side. But it seems that as long as there has been an IT function, we have felt misunderstood and underappreciated. It has always seemed that no matter what we do, we can never truly make our customer happy. At least not for long. And that has meant that we felt that we never really could understand what they wanted.

Here is what I believe. Your customer really does not expect you to perform miracles. Well, not every day anyway. While at times it may seem that they do expect their daily dose of miracles, I believe that most customers are reasonable. They simply want value for their investment. Like me and my relationship with Felix, they want the outcome. They want the pretty, no-fuss yard and they do not want to have to know anything about the details to get it. The problem is that there are now decades of history that established mental models and expectations of the relationship between our customers and us. We have moved further and further apart in our understanding of each other and this disconnect has made it difficult to have a reasonable conversation. It is like two people speaking different languages who, getting frustrated that they cannot understand each other, simply speak louder and louder until they are screaming at one another.

As this paradigm shifts, however, the situation changes. As we begin to solve some of our basic delivery problems, create transparency and offer our customers choice, and cross the line to develop true intimacy with our customers, the relationship transforms. I never expected miracles from Felix. I had a very solid understanding of what was possible and what was not. I understood the costs and risks with every decision. The relationship that we built created a level plane of understanding. The same thing happens in the relationship between IT and its customers as you begin to embody the traits of the Quantum Age.

Unfortunately, many people continue to cling to this belief that customers have unrealistic expectations of their IT organizations. Regardless of how true that may be at any given moment, it is used as an excuse for fatalism and complacency. The mantra goes something like this: "What is the point of trying? 'The business' has unrealistic expectations that we will never be able to meet. It will never be good enough. So why bother?"

As long as this belief is held, nothing will ever change. The lesson of the last few chapters is that we hold the key to our relationship with our customers. We are in control of our own destinies. It is up to us to change the paradigm, to shift the conversation and reshape *our relationship* with *our customers*. If you do that, in good faith, without expecting your customer to immediately jump up and claim you to be the greatest and most awesome IT organization ever known, you will succeed.

It takes patience. It takes a concerted effort over a long period of time to embody and embed these organizational traits. But if you do it with a servant's attitude, seeking to provide value in every interaction, you will see the change happen. Your relationship will be transformed. The tone will change and you will find that you have a partner who does not, in fact, expect miracles at all.

It's a fast, fast world

There is another factor at play here. It is not just our world that is changing. Our customer's world is changing too. While some of the 'unreasonable demand' is a result of the poor relationship and lack of intimacy between us, there is also another source. Some of the reasons our customers seem to place unreasonable demands on us is that unreasonable demands are being placed on them. We are simply no longer living in the world that existed when the modern IT function was born.

We now live in a fast, fast world.

The same factors that have brought us to this point in our relationship with our customers have also had an impact on the relationship that they have with their customers. The pace of business has increased. Consumers' expectations are at an all-time high and their satisfaction with most companies (particularly large companies) is at an all-time low. For the younger generations, the situation is even more acute. So your customers are under increasing pressure to deliver, which creates anxiety and frustration – and all of that gets transferred to you. We can lay this at their feet if we choose to: 'If my customer could get their act together and be able to anticipate these market changes, then they wouldn't have us running these fire drills every month trying to react to each latest thing.'

This is what we do most of the time. But all it does is put a layer of pressure on our customer from both ends of the spectrum. And it erodes our relationship with them. Our customer does not need someone telling them that they need to do a better job of anticipating market changes. They do not need someone who tells them that we cannot react and turn on a dime. They need the opposite. They need a partner who will help them react. A partner who will give them the flexibility to turn on a dime either to answer a competitive threat or to seize a rapidly developing market opportunity. This is the new reality. And they need a partner who can help them live within it.

In order for our customer to survive, they need to react much more quickly and they need the tools that enable them to thrive in a world that is in a state of constant change. Nowhere is this more important than with technology. It is the lifeblood of everything that they do. They need an IT partner who can bring this to the table. They need their IT partner to be dynamic.

Building on the foundation

Customers do not expect miracles. Check. But they are living in a world that is moving faster than ever before and they need our help to react and prosper in this fast, fast world. Check.

Now what?

That may make sense, but it also sounds like we should all just plan on not sleeping, working non-stop until we burn out, and then going and finding another profession. It is a basic law of nature: you cannot run harder and faster forever. Eventually, something will break down. So what are we supposed to do?

The only thing we can. Change our approach.

Everything that we've covered up to this point, if taken in isolation, doesn't seem that dramatic. But when you put it all together, it's much more fundamental. If you don't gloss over it, it represents a completely different approach to how we provide services – and how we see our role in that process. Being dynamic is not quite like the other four traits. The other four traits are the building blocks. The basic skills. Being 'dynamic' is less a skill set than it is an attitude and an approach.

It is a trait that changes how you use the other four traits. You can embody all or parts of the first four traits and still not realize your potential as an organization. If you never put them together and make something new, something bigger from them, then they just become incremental improvements.

... You're supposed to teach and I'm supposed to learn. For four days I've been bustin' my ****, and haven't learned a thing.

In the 1984 movie *The Karate Kid*, the wise master Miyagi tries to teach an impatient young kid the true art of karate. But after a few days, Daniel, the student, gets frustrated. In reply, Miyagi answers, "You learn plenty."

I learn plenty, yeah. I learned how to sand your decks maybe. I washed your car, paint your house, paint your fence. I learn plenty!

Ah, not everything is as seems ...

"I'm going home, man." And Daniel storms off. But Miyagi calls him back. He tells him to "wax the car." As Daniel begins to do the motion, Miyagi strikes at him ... and Daniel blocks it. Miyagi goes on to show him that these seemingly disconnected skills are actually the building blocks that Daniel needed to learn to be able to begin the journey to become a karate master. He realized that he has learned much, but that he had not yet learned how to put them together. He had not yet learned that by changing his perspective and by using them differently, he could use them to achieve something greater.

It is the same with the first four traits. Becoming a learning organization is important. Building discipline if foundational. Instilling transparency and developing intimacy are vital to building the necessary relationship with your customer. But by themselves, none of them are enough. They must all be brought together and turned into something more. They must be used as the catalyst to change the fundamental posture of who we are as professionals, of who we are as teams and who we are as organizations.

From the old, the new

If we must build the traits of becoming a Learning, Disciplined, Transparent and Intimate Organization and then use them to fundamentally change who we are and how we see ourselves, what does that look like? It can be difficult to imagine something fundamentally different from the reality that you've always lived. It can also be deceiving. Because, on the surface, it may not look all that different. But becoming a dynamic organization in the Quantum Age will have less to do with what the IT organization 'looks' like and more with what it 'feels' like.

The first thing is that the dynamic organization will be entirely customer-focused. There will be no value placed on technology or even service in or for itself. They will merely be the vehicles. Like any well-run business, the dynamic organization is one that is driven from a customer-centric core. At every level of the organization, in all aspects of operation, the first frame of reference will always be the customer. This is because it is only from this frame of reference that you can effectively utilize the other four traits.

OK, everybody, thanks for joining today's meeting to discuss a potential network upgrade. Veronica, can you please walk us through the business case. What is the customer need driving this request and what is the expected value that we are to deliver?

This may sound a bit strange, but this is where every conversation in a dynamic organization begins. If it doesn't, then you cannot possibly harness the new traits of the organization. While the four foundational traits are developed from the 'bottom up,' beginning with learning and building to intimacy, they are applied in reverse.

There are several new initiatives planned for next year, within both our consumer products division and the retail operations division, that we are projecting will increase network utilization by 40–60% over a period of three months. We had several conversations with customers in both divisions and we believe that these will be sustained increases based on the new interfaces and the associated marketing campaigns. Our projections are further showing that under sustained impact, it will result in a slowdown of customer transactions by 10–20% and that the potential cost in terms of market perception far outweighed the cost to upgrade the network to avoid these costs. We have looked at the rest of the components of the supply chain – the servers, middleware components, and application elements – and we believe that they are all capable of handling the increased traffic, so it is only the network components that we are concerned with at this point. So the objective of this effort is to increase our network capacity to mitigate the increased traffic and ensure that we do not see the projected customer transaction slowdown.

There are two primary things to consider in this little bit of fiction. First, this is not a 'network meeting.' This meeting is dealing with the customer's needs and the potential impact on their customers. While the focus has been determined to be on the network, the view is holistic. Nothing is happening in isolation. They are not solely focused on the network. They have looked at all things that would impact on the customer experience and have homed in on the network as the area on which they need to focus. The focus on the network is the end of the process, not the beginning of it. Second, the focus of this meeting is on the potential, the *future*, impact on the customer. They are not reacting. They are projecting.

When you hear the term 'dynamic organization,' you probably have this image of this great organization standing in the middle of chaos. As things fly at you, you deftly swat them away, handling everything with cool confidence. No matter what comes, you react to it. You handle it. But this is not really what it means to be dynamic. A dynamic organization is only rarely reactive. Its primary posture is proactive.

Have you ever seen someone perform who you would consider a true professional? Do you notice how they make everything they do look so simple. Everything that they do is so smooth and seemingly effortless that they lull you into looking right past their excellence.

As a kid, I took piano lessons. I remember watching someone play Rachmaninoff's *Rhapsody on a Theme of Paganini*, 18th Variation. It was so beautiful, so melodic. It was slow and seemed so deliberate. The person playing it looked so calm and, well, happy when they were playing. They made it look and sound so simple. So I figured I could play it too. Then I saw the sheet music. It was anything but simple. Despite its relatively slow pacing, it was intricate. It required a tremendous amount of balance in the playing.

Greatness does not just happen. It takes training. It takes practice. It is rarely reactive in the raw sense. It only seems that way. I remember watching the U.S. Tennis Open one year when Roger Federer made this amazing shot. He had approached the net and his opponent hit a lob over his head. He ran it down, but was not going to have time to turn and return it, so he came over it and hit a winner from between his legs. It looked like an amazing stroke of luck. The spur-of-the-moment reaction that only a pro of great natural talent could make. We excitedly discussed it the next morning with our tennis coach:

"Did you see that amazing shot that Federer made yesterday?" I asked John.

"Yeah, that was great, wasn't it? That is why he practices shots like those."

"He practices that kind of shot?"

"Of course he does. He knows that he might need to react to something like that at some point, so he practices it. He practices everything."

That is the sign of a true professional – either as an individual or as an organization. Nothing is left to chance. Reaction is only the last stage of a very long, proactive process of preparation. That is why the first four traits serve as the building blocks of becoming a dynamic organization. They represent the practice, the discipline, and the insight that you need to become anticipatory. They enable you to move quickly, to react, to adapt, and to adopt. They enable you to innovate rapidly. They enable you to be dynamic.

The attributes of the dynamic organization

In this fast, fast world, your customer needs you to be dynamic. They need a partner who can help them react swiftly to market changes, one who can help them seize rapidly materializing opportunities. They need a dynamic organization that can help them do this by embodying four key attributes. They need an organization that is:

- Fast and Reactive
- Flexible and Adaptive
- Adoptive (living in the customer's world)

- Innovative.

These attributes are what make up the new IT organization. They represent what we must become. They represent what we will become as we become dynamic.

Fast and reactive

The starting point for a dynamic organization is to *appear* fast and reactive to your customer. The word 'appear' may not be quite fair. It is not that you are fooling them in any way. But, as I hope I have made clear so far in this chapter, what appears to be reactive is actually the result of a very proactive approach. So while the goal is not to be reactive in the true sense of the word, from your customer's perspective your organization should be seen as both fast and reactive.

Being fast and reactive is predominately built on the back of the first two traits. The extent to which you are successful in building a learning and disciplined organization will largely determine the degree to which you are perceived to be fast and reactive. Like Daniel in *The Karate Kid*, being fast and reactive is all about training, balance and committing repetitive actions to 'muscle memory.' By continually refining and improving processes and building the organizational discipline that enables your organization to function seamlessly, you will create this kind of fast and reactive organization. Routine requests will become, well, routine.

But being fast and reactive requires at least a small dose and application of both transparency and intimacy. To appear reactive, you must be proactive. This is a key part of maturing your discipline. By creating deliberate and continual dialogue with your customer, you will almost always see (or at least sense) what is coming and, therefore, will be much better prepared to react to it. At one point in my father's career, he was the watch commander of a sheriff's station in Los Angeles. As he pulled into the station one afternoon, he had an uneasy feeling. He told his sergeants during the shift briefing that he wanted the riot gear in every squad car double-checked. Sure enough, there were some significant issues that evening and the riot gear was required to respond to the situation.

At the end of the shift, his sergeants pulled him aside and asked him how he knew that something would happen that evening. He told them that he hadn't known. Something just told him that everything should be double-checked. As he reflected on the situation later, he put it together. The Santa Ana winds were blowing that evening and it had been an unusually warm day. His subconscious had registered that this combination often led to restless people eager to let off steam and cause some trouble. When the situation hit, he and his teams had been able to react rapidly. Much of it was their training and discipline. But part of it was that my father was able to sense that a situation might be brewing. By building transparency and intimacy with your customer, you will enable the same kind of response.

This is the leap that you must be willing to make if you are to become a dynamic organization. You must focus on and build discipline and intimacy. But you must then be willing to trust the intuition that they will create. If there is one thing that cripples IT organizations as they attempt to build this type of rigor, it is that they allow it to become bureaucratic. They allow it to take the place of human intuition. If you build a learning organization that is always improving and becomes accustomed to constant change, if you build high levels of discipline and rigor, and if you have created consistent dialogue and deep levels of intimacy with your customer, then you will have done what you need to do. At that point, you and your team will know what needs to happen. You will sense it. It will be in your organizational muscle memory. At that point, you simply need to learn to trust it and let it go.

Flexible and adaptive

Speed and rapid reactions are what most people think of when the term 'dynamic organization' is mentioned. That is the best starting point. Frankly, most enterprises would be ecstatic if they could refer to their IT organization as 'fast and reactive' with a straight face. But while that is a great start, it really isn't enough. Being reactive still only implies that the organization is operating largely within the parameters that were originally established. It assumes that the general scope of operations remains unchanged. But in the fast, fast world we are living in, that is not always the case. Sometimes, being fast is not enough. Sometimes the game itself changes.

In those situations, your customer needs something more from you. They need you to be able to change course quickly. They need you to be flexible. They need you to be able to adapt to the changing circumstance. More to the point, they need you to be flexible enough to help *them* adapt to whatever the market has thrown at them. But how can you be flexible and adaptive? What does that mean?

Being a flexible and adaptive organization really requires two things. First, it will be built upon the foundation of being a learning and disciplined organization. By instilling the discipline of a learning organization, your team will be accustomed to constant change and evolution. You will have removed the normal state of inertia which exists in most organizations and which is the single largest barrier to flexibility. In addition, with high levels of discipline instilled within your organization, your teams will understand how to follow each other's lead. Remember that true discipline is not about blindly following the rules. It is about applying effective judgment to get a repeatable result. That skill set will also allow your team to move as a team – even if it is moving in another direction.

The second thing that a flexible and adaptive organization requires, though, is a bit tougher. It requires creativity and the freedom to take risks. In most organizations, creativity and risk taking are removed from the organization like a cancer. In the dynamic organization, they are in abundance. It is the freedom to take risks and the visible commitment to instilling creativity at all levels of the organization that, on top of learning and discipline, will create flexibility and adaptability. Conversely, it is the fear of risk and the lack of creative cognition that holds most IT organizations back from achieving this type of dynamic culture.

When people are afraid to apply critical thinking skills and explore creative solutions to challenging problems, and when they believe that the personal risk of trying something new is too great, they will simply play it safe with the tried and true responses to any situation. To become a dynamic organization, you need to break this cycle. At each and every level you need to encourage and celebrate creativity. You need to encourage smart risk taking. If you have built a true learning organization, the actual risk is minimal. Silly mistakes will not be repeated. Every misfire will be a lesson learned. And with every step, your team will become ever more confident in their ability to have significant and dramatic positive impacts on their customers.

This is the secret of creating a flexible and adaptive organization: creating that perfect mix of creativity and smart risk taking, built upon the foundation of a highly disciplined organization that is committed to constant improvement and evolution.

Adoptive (living in the customer's world)

Is it enough? Being fast, reactive, flexible, and adaptive? It is a huge chunk of what it means to be a dynamic organization. But no, it is not enough. The reason is that these attributes of the dynamic organization are still based on the assumption that your customer can tell you what is needed. All four of these attributes are founded on the customer placing a demand upon IT and IT's ability to respond – whether reactively or proactively. It is true that if most IT organizations did this consistently – were truly fast and reactive, flexible and adaptive – then the entire relationship would be different.

But the world is changing around us and it simply will not be enough as we move forward. As the world gets ever faster and technology seeps ever deeper into the core of every transaction and every experience, your customer will simply not be able to anticipate and dictate every need. They simply will not know what they need or when they will need it.

In 2004, Malcolm Gladwell, the author of several books, including *The Tipping Point* and *Blink*, gave a presentation at a TED conference in Monterey, California. In this presentation, Gladwell told the story of Howard Muskowitz and his experience with spaghetti sauce. In this story, Muskowitz was hired by Campbells, who owned the Prego brand of pasta sauces. For years, Campbells had done market research and run focus groups and they all told them the same thing – people wanted a traditional, thin pasta sauce. So that is what they made. But they lagged behind Ragu and were trying to find something that would make the difference. Enter Muskowitz. Rather than simply ask people what they wanted, he had the Prego kitchens cook up over 45 different versions of pasta sauce in every imaginable combination of consistency and taste. Then they set out on a road trip and simply had people try the different sauces and tell them which they liked. What they discovered was that there were actually three clusters of people who liked different kinds of pasta sauce: those who liked traditional sauce, those who liked it spicy and those who liked it extra chunky. This meant that a third of America wanted an extra chunky pasta sauce, but they didn't even know it. So, of course, they couldn't ask for it.

Steve Jobs, CEO of Apple, instinctively understood this. When he was asked how much market research he did before he created the iPad, he responded, "None. It's not the consumers' job to know what they want." He knew that he couldn't rely on his customers to be able to imagine capabilities that did not yet exist. He created new technologies that were fundamentally the things that he wished existed, that he would want if he were the consumer. Which, of course, he was. It was often said that no one was more amazed and delighted with Apple's products than was Jobs.

Of course, Steve Jobs was not like the rest of us. He had an amazing vision of what technology could do and how it could be applied in ways that the rest of us simply couldn't see. But his gift was to be able to put himself in our shoes. To see the possibilities from our perspective – from a future perspective that we didn't yet have, but would have. That is what it means to be adoptive. It is more than merely being empathetic. It is more than having a good and close relationship with your customer. That still keeps you separate from them. Close, maybe, but separate. To be adoptive is to become one with your customer. In fact, the Latin root of the word means to 'select for oneself.' To be adoptive is to voluntarily cross the line, to choose to adopt your customer's perspectives, attitudes, and viewpoints. It is only from this position that you can truly understand your customer and become a dynamic organization.

Becoming adoptive begins with transparency and intimacy. Offering honest choice and open dialogue, and building a relationship, is the bridge. But becoming adoptive means crossing the bridge. You have a choice. You each can stand on either side of the bridge and exchange ideas. Or you can cross it, adopt the customer's positions as your own and operate from within their worldview. It's the difference between being friendly neighbors and being family.

This can be a tough line to cross. It means sacrificing a huge chunk of your identity. But do you really want an identity separate from that of your customer? Being adoptive obliterates the line between you and your customer. You cease to be a mere 'service provider' and instead are the 'inside guy.' You cannot begin to consider being adoptive without the foundation of a deeply trusting relationship. That is the foundation that the first four traits build. They will have built the bridge. They will have opened the door. But it is that door that you must walk through if you are to become a fully dynamic organization.

Innovative

Innovation has become such a common word. Its ubiquity, however, belies its power. Because it is thrown out so often and so freely, people have forgotten what it really means to be innovative. To be innovative is to create something new, something original. It implies deep levels of creativity. Innovation is not adding a new feature or doing something a little bit differently. To innovate is to create something that breaks the rules that everyone else is playing by right now. It changes the game.

Unfortunately, most IT organizations have forgone their opportunity to innovate. They have willingly left the right to innovate to others outside the organization. We have allowed ourselves to become caretakers. We have allowed to take root the myth that we lack either the ability or the resources to innovate. So we have busied ourselves with the urgent matters of the day, which in the end are just not that meaningful.

You may be getting upset right about now. 'We innovate,' you may be thinking to yourself. But what was the last innovation that changed the game for your customer? What completely reshaped the business, the competitive landscape, or the approach to the market? If there was that type of innovation, how involved was IT? In most cases, there is no answer to these questions. It is just not what most IT organizations do in today's world.

But it does not need to be so.

If you have built the first four traits, if you have become fast and reactive, flexible and adaptive, and if you have adopted your customer's worldview as your own, then there will be no one – no one – in a better position to drive game-changing innovation in your organization. No one. That level of engagement, that level of intimacy, that level of completely merging your organizational being into the fabric of the company will give you access to insights and vision that no one else within or outside the organization will possess. And from that perch, there will be no one else better positioned to lead innovation that changes everything.

Frankly, this is less of an attribute to be developed than it is a promise. If you have faithfully gone down this road, developed the first four traits and then made the choices that you need to make to become a dynamic organization, then this kind of game-changing innovation is the natural by-product. You really cannot avoid it. It will simply be who you are as an organization.

The IT organization you and your customer always wanted

The new Vice President of Marketing enters her office. It is the first day of the new job and she wonders if it was all a good sales job on her. Would the reality live up to the hype? During her round of interviews, she had met with the CIO, who frankly blew her away. He described how they were organized into a set of 'service lines' designed to meet the needs of specific customer segments. Two of those service lines were specific to the services that her group required. Some were services that were utilized across the enterprise. He described how he had a team of his people embedded within her organization, working alongside her team to ensure that IT's services were being leveraged most effectively to help achieve the organization's strategic marketing objectives. He showed her the online tool that enabled her to see which services were being consumed by her group and at what cost, and the how they were impacting her services and goals. And they were in terms that meant something to her – nothing about 'up-time' and 'number of incidents.'

She loved it. Her first thought was that this was someplace that she could finally stop fighting the battles just to get obstacles out of the way and actually get something done. But she was afraid to get her hopes up too high. It just seemed too good to be true. Could the IT organization really function that way? Was it really possible?

As she walked into the office, there was a small box with a note attached sitting on her desk. She opened the box and found a small figure of a world with four human shapes interlocked around it. The inscription at the base said, "Together We Can Change the World." The attached note read:

Ms. Washington,

My name is Frank Larkin and I am your chief IT advocate. The small figure is a gift that our organization produced to remind all of us that we are all in this together and that only together can we achieve great things. I hope that you like it.

I am sure that as you get settled, you will have some questions and perhaps need some things immediately. Your laptop has been configured as you requested during the employment process and you have been granted access to all systems that you should need. There is on-demand training available for all systems that you will be accessing; however, I will also be happy to schedule you for traditional, in-person training or to arrange for one-on-one training if you prefer. We believe that everything should be set up to enable you to jump right into things; however, should anything be missing or if you have any questions, please feel free to call me on my mobile at 949-555-1212.

Finally, I have sent you a meeting request for lunch later this week. If that day does not work for you, please let me know when would be more convenient for you. I would like us to spend time simply getting to know one another and to begin understanding your goals and plans for the organization as they develop so that I can most appropriately direct your embedded teams and ensure that we are prepared to support your plans fully.

I am looking forward to working with you as we achieve success together!

Until later this week,

Frank

* * *

Talking to his brother last night, James was reminded how most of the rest of the world lived. He had almost forgotten. His brother had called to get his opinion on a new engineering application that his company was considering. As part of the conversation, James' brother launched into a 30-minute rant on his horrible IT organization.

"All they ever say is no," he said. "If I didn't know better, I would swear that they were paid to try to get me to stop using technology. I just cringe anytime I need to do anything that involves IT. It is always the most painful part of my day. Most of the time, I would rather just deal with the junky technology than bother trying to interact with them at all."

James really did not know what to tell him. He consoled him the best he could, gave him his opinion on the application and then switched the topic to plans for their next get-together. He did not dare tell him how things worked at his company. How he had almost completely forgotten experiences like that. Now, working with IT was his favorite thing in the world. His interactions were nothing like his brother's. When he interacted with IT, he always came away hopeful and energized. His IT group (that's how he thought of them – as 'his'), understood him. Most of the time, when he met them, it barely felt like they were meeting about IT at all. They were always talking about the challenges that his engineering team was facing. Where there were risks and opportunities – not from an IT perspective, but from his perspective. His IT team would talk about some things that they had learned about how another engineering group was approaching a problem or they would brainstorm together about some new ideas he was working on.

The word 'no' never really came into the question. It was not a game where he begged for something and they told him whether or not he could have it. They just talked. It was like they were his business partners. Like they were inside his head. They knew what was going on and always had an idea to share and hands to get dirty to help him out. He had no doubt that he was able to get so much more done and have a much greater impact because of his relationship with IT. He knew one thing: he was never going back to an organization like his brother's. That would be a fate worse than death.

* * *

Sonya picked up the phone and called the Service Desk. She caught herself smiling. After a few moments she heard, "Thank you for calling the Service Desk. This is Tom and I am pleased to be of service to you today. Is this Sonya?"

"Yes it is."

"Great. I see that we did an upgrade on your system last night. It looks like everything worked fine, but did you run into a problem with it?"

"No. It all went great. I actually was just calling to say thanks for handling the situation. I didn't even know that something was wrong. It was awesome that you were able to catch it and fix it before I even noticed. I got an email from Micha Williams that explained what had happened and everything she had done. I completed the little survey, but I just felt that it deserved a call to say 'thank you.'"

"Well, I'm very glad to hear that – and you're welcome. It's always gratifying when we're able to solve a problem before it has become a problem. I'll make sure that Micha and her boss know that you called. I'm sure that she'll be very happy about it."

"That's wonderful. Thank you. While I have you on the phone, there is one other thing, uh, if you still have a moment."

"Of course. What is it?"

"I was reading this book last night – it's a murder mystery – and the main character actually works in finance, like me. Well, sort of like me. You know they always make things so much more exciting in those books. Anyway, in the book she used something called an analytics tool to do some quick what-if analysis. It made me think. Something like that would be very useful with my job. Do we have something like that here? I didn't want to be foolish and ask a stupid question, but you guys are always so nice and you know everything that's going on, I figured that I could ask you."

"Hmmm. Let me see. Hang on a moment. Actually, depending on what kind of data you are trying to work with, there are a couple of options. The first is a local data analyzer tool. It's actually an add-on to Excel and it's something that's available to you with manager approval. If you mostly work with local, Excel-based data, it might do the trick. If that sounds right, I can schedule a virtual walk-through of the tool with you so that you can see if it might work. And if so, we would also be happy to join a call or meeting with your manager to explain how this tool might be helpful in your situation. If you're looking at working with data directly in the financial system, there is also a pilot under way right now. I could check to see if your group is involved."

"No, no. I am working with local data, so the first option sounds perfect. Could we set up that walk-through? This could be something that really helps me."

After scheduling the walk-through, Sonya thanked Tom and hung up. Almost immediately, she received a follow-up email confirming the walk-through; an introduction from Tom to Dean, who would be doing the walk-through; and a PDF that provided a high-level overview of the tool and the ways that groups within the company were already using it.

Sonya smiled again. The fact that IT was able to solve a problem before she even knew about it was great. But what was really awesome was that she felt that there was someone on her side. Someone she could turn to about technology without feeling foolish or stupid. They treated her with such respect and really showed that they cared about her and her job and wanted to do everything that they could to help her to do it better. She loved where she worked.

* * *

These three vignettes may sound like fantasy to you. Pure fairytale. In today's world, they are largely just a dream. But I believe that there are only two options as we enter the Quantum Age. Become this organization – or cease to exist. Any IT organization that does not become this type of organization will simply be removed from the equation. Companies will simply decide that they can get service that is like this – or at least a lot closer to this and at much less cost – from the outside. And they will go there. Unfortunately, however, it will be to their own detriment. Because I also believe that no outside organization will ever deliver the amount of value for them that a Quantum IT organization can deliver.

An IT organization that embraces the five organizational traits – that becomes a Learning, Disciplined, Transparent, Intimate, and, finally, Dynamic Organization – can and will become the type of organization described in these stories. If you suspend the cynicism for a moment, if you forget all of the historical and political baggage for a few short minutes, you will realize that the distance between your current reality and this vision is really not that far. It is actually not that difficult to imagine a scenario in which these types of interaction can occur.

But, to do so, we must overcome our history. We must break the molds, the mental models and the habits that have held us in a state of inertia. We must let go of our pride and need for recognition and approach our customer with humility, vulnerability, and a genuine desire to serve. We must commit ourselves to continually improving, to never being satisfied, to instilling rigor, to being brutally honest and open, to being trusting, and to going into each interaction with a relational mindset rather than a transactional mindset. We must leverage all of this to become fast and flexible and we must cross the bridge to make our customer's worldview the only view that matters. If we do all of these things, if we're willing to envision ourselves, our roles, and our entire organizations in a new light, we can and we will become the IT organization that our customer always wanted us to become.

And the organization that we always knew we could be.

Chapter 9 key points

Becoming a Dynamic Organization represents the pinnacle of our relationship with our customers. It represents a relationship of deep trust and one in which the customer is able to get the value that they seek from their investments with as little friction and pain as possible.

Here are the key points you should remember from this chapter:

- It may sometimes feel as if we can never satisfy our customers, but in truth they do not expect miracles – they just want value.

- If you're patient, if you approach your relationship with a servant's attitude, your relationship will be transformed into a deep and lasting partnership.

- We need to realize that we now live in a fast, fast world and that the demands of the market are putting increasing pressure on our customers – they need a partner who will help them react.

- Becoming a Dynamic Organization is really an approach – it brings together the other four traits in a cohesive manner to change the fundamental posture of the IT organization.

- A Dynamic Organization will be entirely customer-focused.
- To be a Dynamic Organization, we must become:
  - o Fast and Reactive
  - o Flexible and Adaptive
  - o Adoptive (we must live in the customer's world)
  - o Innovative.

PART IV

FIVE SKILLS YOU NEED TO THRIVE IN THE QUANTUM AGE

CHAPTER 10: THE PEOPLE PROBLEM: WHY YOUR TECHNICAL SKILLS WILL WORK AGAINST YOU

In September 2011, Paul LePage decided that he was going to do something about unemployment. The governor of Maine, like many other leaders throughout the country, was faced with an increasingly stubborn problem. He had too many unemployed people in his state. Something needed to be done about it.

The common view is that there are not enough jobs. With all of the layoffs and cutbacks, there is just not enough work to go around. So Governor LePage convened a roundtable discussion of prominent employers from throughout the state, along with experts from places like Harvard, to see what could be done about the situation. What he learned was that the problem was not, in fact, a lack of jobs. It was a lack of skills.

As in many places around the country, businesses in Maine have continued to evolve. In some industries, old positions have been combined to create new positions that have skill requirements that no one in any one of the previous jobs could meet. In Maine, it was discovered that there were almost enough open positions to give every unemployed person in the state a job. The issue was not a lack of jobs. It was a skill gap.

The skills that people had acquired and developed before the recession were no longer the skills that employers needed. The jobless had failed to adapt their skills. They were waiting for a job to utilize the skills they had, when a job was waiting for them if they would only adapt and learn some new skills.

The governor's answer was to create a new program designed specifically to give graduating high-school students who were not going on to a four-year college the skills that they needed to compete in today's market.

The situation is not very different in IT.

As we enter the Quantum Age, the skills needed within IT organizations are shifting. As we move from a manufacturing paradigm to a retail one, the types of jobs and the skills needed to fulfill those jobs will shift. As we move away from a one-size-fits-all 'Walstroms' approach to a more refined Strategic Sourcer or Strategic Innovator model, the skills needed will get more specific and more targeted.

There's one more thing. Those skills will not be technical. The technical skills will still be there. They will still be needed. But they will be the ante – the cost to enter the game. The problem is that it will take a while for these skill gaps to become obvious. As the group of government and business leaders in Maine learned, the skill gap develops like a robber in the night, slowly taking away the vitality of a community without them realizing it. Then, one day, people wake up and realize that they are no longer qualified for their own job, let alone any other.

You have the opportunity to avoid this fate. There is no Governor LePage for IT who will create a simple program for you to follow, but there is a way. You will need to take it upon yourself to learn some new skills. You will need to prepare yourself for the coming transition. Your future is within your grasp. You must simply be willing to recognize that standing still, resting on your current skills, is a road to nowhere. Then be willing to step out onto another road. One that leads into the Quantum Age.

The myth of organizational transformation

This book basically tells the story of the organizational transformation that must occur within every IT organization. There is one small problem with this. It is a myth. There is no such thing as an organizational transformation. Organizations are structures, groups of people that voluntarily form (for compensation or otherwise) to fulfill some purpose. They are not living, breathing organisms in and of themselves. While we often talk about them as such, talk about an organization's mission or culture, all of these are simply reflections of the people who make up the organization. Everything that happens within the state of an organization, every interaction, every transaction, every decision, every good thing, and every bad thing – all of them are built, executed, or guided in some way by a human.

Even though it may feel it at times, no organization has a spirit or a soul. There is no such thing as organizational behavior. There are only individual behaviors. They may adhere to a cultural norm that exists within the culture of an organization, but in the end an individual takes each action. My behavior is my own. I may cop out and say that I was only adhering to the cultural norm or doing what everyone else did, but I still had to choose to act.

We often talk about organizations in this sense as a matter of convenience. It offers us a simple way to generalize – a way to discuss the whole of the situation so that we can see the big picture and make sweeping decisions. That's a good thing. And it's true that an organization's culture can predict for us how people will act. We can infer the decisions that people will make, the attitudes that people will hold, and the reaction that people will have to something by understanding the organization's culture. Making decisions ignoring the organization's culture is a recipe for failure. Failing to understand the underlying cultural norms that will dictate these perceptions and values leaves us vulnerable to reactions that were completely predictable.

While operating at an organizational level can be a very useful tool in understanding and predicting reactions and behavior across large groups of people, it can also lull us into believing that we can affect change at that level. Because we're able to see behavior and attitudes across this broad swath, we mistakenly begin to believe that the group is homogeneous – that we can, in fact, change the behavior of the group, as a group. In order to see these cultural norms, we reduce people to personas, and we come to believe that, like chess pieces on a board, we can simply move that persona in any way we choose.

It is a fatal mistake.

There is no such thing as organizational transformation. Transformation is always personal. It is always individual. It also can only be realized from the inside out. That is, you cannot transform another person. You can only transform yourself. As a manager or executive, the best you can hope for is to offer people a reason to change and the tools and opportunity to make it possible. But you cannot force them to change. You cannot make them change. You cannot foist a transformation upon them. It can only happen if someone chooses it. Transformation only occurs if you choose to transform yourself.

Let that sink in for a minute.

Everything presented in this book up to this point has been at the macro level – what needs to happen organizationally. You may have seen yourself as an observer in this process, wondering how all of this will affect you. But this is not abstract. This is where it gets personal. Right here. Right now. If transformation cannot happen organizationally, if it is always personal, always individual, then that means that you are not an innocent bystander.

This is all about you.

In fact, it is all up to you.

Cooking up the five traits

That is a bit sobering, isn't it?

If you're an executive, you might have felt a sense of responsibility for leading your team through this transition. But if you were a service desk agent, a programmer, a network engineer, or a database administrator you may have been sitting there chuckling to yourself a bit. Thinking, 'Boy, I guess I'm glad that I'm not responsible for leading everyone through this mess.' Perhaps you continued reading to figure out what new skills you might need to learn, but you weren't expecting this, were you?

This section is not *just* about the fact that you need to learn some new skills to remain competitive and relevant as IT transitions. It is bigger than that. Much bigger. Let me net it out: IT will only succeed in completing this transition, will only enter the Quantum Age, if you and everyone around you learns these new skills.

Without you, without your commitment to change how you see your role, without your willingness to learn new skills, your IT organization will wither away. And everyone will lose. It's a lot of weight to carry, I know. But it must be done. There is much more at stake here than just your job. We all must be willing to do this, to do it together. It is the only way.

You must choose to transform. You must choose to step forward and change.

The reason why this is so critical is that the five organizational traits, like an organization's culture, are not real. There is no point at which you can look at an organization and definitely say, 'Yep, they're a learning organization,' or, 'See them, they're an intimate organization.' I'm sure that someone will attempt to create some kind of maturity assessment around this, but these traits are not objective. They are not meant to be objectively defined and measured any more than saying that someone is loyal, courageous, or kind can be precisely measured or defined. You know it when you see it, when you feel it.

More to the point, it is not actually an organization that can possess these traits, any more than you can call an organization kind or loyal. These traits are a reflection. They are a reflection of the people who make up the organization. They are a reflection of those traits living within the individuals of the organization. It's only when those traits are reflected and multiplied, when they become the new cultural norm, that you'll begin to see the organization as a whole possessing those traits. But even at that point, it will still be nothing more than a reflection.

10: The People Problem

You see it now, don't you?

In order for your organization to become a Learning, Disciplined, Transparent, Intimate, and Dynamic Organization, you must first become a learning, disciplined, transparent, intimate, and dynamic individual. That might be a bit tough to digest. That is because we don't really describe people in these terms – at least not exactly. More significantly, it's difficult to say to yourself, 'OK, this is on me. It's all up to me. That means that tomorrow, I will begin to become a learning, disciplined, and transparent individual.' Good luck with that.

It's a bit like waking up one day and realizing that you don't like the fact that people see you as uncaring. You know that you really care about people. You're not some coldhearted loser. So you decide to change. Do you get up the next morning and simply tell yourself that you're going to become more caring? Well, it's a start, but it'll only take you so far. After all, if you knew what that meant and how to do it, you probably wouldn't be in this situation to start with. Instead, you would begin to think about some specific things that make people feel that you're not caring. Perhaps it's that you don't thank people very often. You don't expect people to thank you when you do something that you believe is your responsibility anyway, so you don't think to thank others. Then that is what you may choose to focus on. Saying 'thank you.' That is much more direct, much more tangible, than simply 'being more caring.' In actuality, it is a new skill that you are choosing to learn. You are recognizing that by developing this skill it will enable you to appear (and probably genuinely be) more caring.

It's the same situation with the five traits. They may be a reflection of the organization – and there are some things that will need to happen at an organizational level – but it is up to each and every one of us to embody these traits. To do this, we need to develop some specific skills that will enable us to do so. You can think of it as a recipe for a scrumptious cake. We know what we are trying to create: we want a cake that is moist, fluffy, and complex on the palette, that feels like velvet in the mouth. Those are the characteristics, the 'traits,' of the cake we are trying to create. But we can't just wish that cake into being. There is a process that must be followed.

The recipe itself describes how the ingredients must be put together in the right amounts and in the right order. It describes the specific technique that should be applied at each step of the process to get the desired result. All of that is what the last section of this book describes. It is the recipe and the technique.

But, as any chef will tell you, when it comes to producing a great dish, nothing takes the place of great ingredients. You can have an amazing recipe and superb technique in the kitchen, but if you start with horrible ingredients there is just not much you'll be able to do.

Your skills – and the skills of everyone in IT – are the ingredients. They are the raw product. They are the starting point. Nothing great can be created within the organization without first ensuring that we have the very best ingredients to work with. That is why your personal transformation is so important in this process. Everything that we have discussed up to this point will be built upon these new skills. It is up to you to build and develop them, to create the finest raw ingredients that you can, so that they can be put together to create your own Quantum IT organization.

'What got you here won't get you there'

I can almost see the look on your face. 'Really? You're seriously now telling me not only that my job and how I do it are going to change, but that I have to learn a whole new set of skills?' You're probably right now either completely discounting this and just ignoring it or teetering on despair and figuring that you should just start considering a new profession now. If you're in the first camp, all I can tell you is that you're wrong. You ignore this at your own peril. The importance of the five skills (which we will get to in a minute) – and the significant downplaying of technical skills – is happening right now.

Ashwin Rangan, CIO of Edwards Lifesciences, says of his direct reports, "none of them are technologists. They are relationship managers." Joe Pleasant, CIO at Premier, puts it this way: "If you're a technologists and that's all you know, then you can't survive ... in an [IT] organization. You need to understand analytics and how to communicate and collaborate – both within IT and outside of it." If you believe that you will be able to compete and survive relying solely on your technical skills, your potential job market will shrink considerably. And it will likely not include any but the very largest IT organizations. The technology skills that have been in high demand are being commoditized. There is only one way to see this – those skills are not your future.

If you're in the other camp and just feel that it's all too much, don't despair. It really is not as bad as it may seem at first glance. It's just that we have to recognize that as the situation changes and evolves, we have no choice but to change and evolve with it. These skills are not necessarily difficult to master, but, to some degree, they do run counter to everything that got you to where you are now – and that is the biggest obstacle you must overcome.

In his book *What Got You Here Won't Get You There*, Marshall Goldsmith explains that even in markets that are not going through the level of transition and turmoil that IT is going through, this is a common challenge.

My job is not to make them smarter or richer. My job is to help them – to identify a personal habit that's annoying their coworkers and to help them eliminate it – so that they retain their value to the organization. My job is to make them see that the skills and habits that have taken them this far might not be the right skills and habits to take them further.

Marshall Goldsmith, from *What Got You Here Won't Get You There*

It's not that your skills are bad. They are what got you to where you are – and that's good. But even in normal circumstances they can turn from something that is good into something that is constricting. Goldsmith goes on to explain that as humans we begin to mistake our actions as the sole reason for our success. We begin to overvalue our contributions, to overstate our value, and we fail to recognize the contributions of those around us. Over time, these develop into a series of habits that become destructive – to the organization, but mostly to ourselves. Our relative success blinds us to the reality of how others see us. It blinds us to the impact that our actions are having on others. It is only by recognizing this that we are able to change and become more than we are today.

10: The People Problem

Goldsmith is talking on a personal level and it is certainly true for almost all of us at that level. I know that it's true for me. But it is also true in another way. For all of the complaining that IT is underappreciated, the reality is that almost all IT organizations have a lot of success under their belts. In a very brief span of time, IT organizations and the technology we have delivered have fundamentally changed almost all aspects of the way business is done. Part of the reason we get frustrated is that we know this and feel that we should get greater recognition for these contributions. But it is this very success that can blind us to our own deficiencies. This happens at a 'corporate' level, but also at an individual one. You think to yourself, 'I've been doing this for a long time. I know what I'm doing. If they don't see that and trust me, then that's their problem.'

We become blinded to how our customers see us. We become blinded to the impact that our habits are having on others. We mistake our actions and our habits as the sole reason for our personal success and for the success of the organization. We begin to believe that if what we've done up to this point has gotten us this far, then it should be good enough to carry us through. But it won't. As Goldsmith says, *what got us here, will not get us there.* We must be willing to recognize and admit that things are not as they must be, that change is needed, that our skills and habits simply will not be sufficient to embody the five organizational traits of the Quantum Age.

The truth is that you know this. I believe that it's hard not to know it. We see it happening around us every day. We complain that our customers are expecting too much from us – code for, 'Can't they just leave us alone.' We can feel, almost taste, the tension levels rising. With every meeting, with every new project that spins out of control, it gets worse. But we're more afraid of the unknown than we are of the pain that we find ourselves living in today. There are, of course, those who do not get it. They plod along blissfully doing their technical work, oblivious or outright defiant. IT is a technical domain. Period. My guess is that you are not one of these people. If you were, I doubt that you would have even picked up this book, let alone gotten this far. So you know that this transition must happen. You know that the days of technical skills being the primary criteria for success and respect are coming to an end. You know.

The question is, what, then, are the new skills that must be learned?

Five skills (and three questions) that are the keys to your future

The technical skills that got you here are not going to be the skills that take you into the Quantum Age. Hopefully, I have made that point! But then, what skills do you need? Specifically, there are five of them. I will go into the five skills in the next chapter, but, as you will see, they are the opposite of technical skills. They might be best described as business skills. They represent the specific building blocks that will be required to build the five organizational traits. They are not random. They are also not meant to be comprehensive – that is, they do not represent the only skills that you need. But they are the five critical skills that will accomplish two things:

- provide you the skills you need to be competitive and relevant as the focus of IT changes, and

- provide your organization with the key 'ingredients' that are needed to complete this transition successfully.

They represent the key to both your future and the future of your organization. There may be nothing more important than developing these skills in yourself and in those around you. The next chapter will discuss each of these skills in detail. I know that you want to get to them, but be patient. Because before we get to them, there is one more thing that we need to cover. One more prerequisite. Call it a 'super skill.' It may be more than a skill; it's an understanding. One of the greatest challenges that we all have suffered from as IT professionals is a lack of perspective. Because of our technical nature, because of our love for the technology and its promise, we sometimes forget who we serve and why.

The concept of service is where we must start. We have to get comfortable with the idea that we do, in fact, exist to serve. That can rub some people the wrong way, but I do not believe that there is anything wrong with it. I believe that we are called to be of service to one another and that it only makes sense to carry this forward into our professional lives. The 'super skill,' the understanding, is that we must see ourselves in this light. We must not see the five skills as 'technical skills' that we must seek to master as much as tools to help us fulfill our personal mission to serve our coworkers and customers. You must start from this perspective in order to successfully learn the five skills as they are intended.

In 1903, Leo Tolstoy published a short story called *The Three Questions*. It tells the story of a king who is troubled and wants to discover the answer to his three questions. He believes that if he can learn the answers to these questions, he will always know what to do. He wants to know:

- When is the best time to do each thing?
- Who are the most important people to work with?
- What is the most important thing to do at all times?

It is a parable that can be applied to our situation. And I believe that as we each seek to develop our new skills, we should be asking and contemplating the same three questions. His story and the answers that he discovers can be used to guide us as we move forward into this new era.

The story continues:

Unsatisfied with the answer he gets from his court, he heads off in disguise to discover the answers from a wise, old hermit who lives in the forest. He finds the hermit struggling to plant a garden and decides to help him. After a long time spent working on his garden, a man rushes in from the forest, bleeding from a wound. The king stops the bleeding, nurses him to health overnight, and saves his life. The man, the king comes to find, had been intent on killing him, but had instead been wounded by the king's bodyguard. Unbeknownst to him, the king had saved the life of his would-be assassin. This act of kindness changes the heart of the assassin and they are reconciled. While pleased with the turn of events, the king has now become frustrated that the hermit has still not answered his three questions.

Tolstoy finishes the story:

"You have already been answered!" said the hermit, still crouching on his thin legs, and looking up at the King, who stood before him.

"How answered? What do you mean?" asked the King.

"Do you not see," replied the hermit. "If you had not pitied my weakness yesterday, and had not dug those beds for me, but had gone your way, that man would have attacked you, and you would have repented of not having stayed with me. So the most important time was when you were digging the beds; and I was the most important man; and to do me good was your most important business. Afterwards when that man ran to us, the most important time was when you were attending to him, for if you had not bound up his wounds he would have died without having made peace with you. So he was the most important man, and what you did for him was your most important business.

"Remember, then: there is only one time that is important – Now! It is the most important time because it is the only time when we have any power. The most necessary man is he with whom you are, for no man knows whether he will ever have dealings with anyone else: and the most important affair is, to do him good, because for that purpose alone was man sent into this life!"

As we step out onto this road to begin this journey to develop these five new skills, in search of the building blocks to develop the five organizational traits, we must always remember the 'why' of it all. It can be easy to get caught up in the undertaking. It can be easy to reduce this to a technical process of building a new set of technical skills. But through this process, we must always remember that we are here to serve. There is nothing more important than the customer, coworker, or supplier who is standing in front of you. And there is nothing more important than doing all that you can to serve them.

Chapter 10 key points

The skills needed in the Quantum Age are shifting from what has historically been needed. As we go from being manufacturers to retailers the jobs needed in this environment will change. They will be much less technical and much more business-oriented.

Here are the key points you should remember from this chapter:

- There is no such thing as organizational transformation. Transformation is always personal.
- You can only transform yourself – which means that it's all up to you.
- IT will only succeed in completing this transition, will only enter the Quantum Age, if you and everyone around you learns these new skills.
- Organizational traits are merely a reflection of those traits living within the individuals of the organization.
- The days of technical skills being the primary criteria for success and respect are coming to an end.
- IT professionals need the proper perspective – we exist to serve.

CHAPTER 11: FIVE SKILLS EVERY IT PROFESSIONAL NEEDS NOW

You can't teach an old dog new tricks.

Ancient proverb

That is what learning is. You suddenly understand something you've understood all your life, but in a new way.

Doris Lessing

If you hold a cat by the tail, you learn things that you cannot learn any other way.

Mark Twain

Learning something new can be one of the most exciting things in the world. Learning something new can be one of the scariest things in the world. A lot of times, it is both. And, as Mark Twain points out in his colorful way, in many cases there is simply no other way to learn than by doing something.

As we dive into the five skills that you must learn, that is an important point to understand. This is not about 'book learning.' I doubt very much that there will be much of anything that you find in this chapter that you haven't already heard and don't already know. The challenge, therefore, is not simply to learn. Instead, it is to:

• understand how these skills fit together and their connection to your new role, and

• put them into practice.

The goal of this chapter is to help you meet this challenge. First, as we go through these skills, the objective is to help you see these five areas in a new light. Leadership, as an example, is a topic that has been written about extensively. It is a term that has been bandied about endlessly. So, are you exhibiting leadership in your day-to-day work? What does that even mean? The purpose of this chapter is to take each of these five skill areas and to break them down into something that is tangible and meaningful in the context of the day-to-day life of an IT professional.

The next step will be up to you. You need to do something. You need to put these skills into practice. Toward the end of this book, there is a "Practical Guide to Getting Started," which will provide some specific step-by-step guidance on how to get started. But in this chapter, we will provide some guidance on what it actually means to put these skills into practice and what that should look like as you dive in.

These skills can only be learned by doing them. Reading this chapter is the first, small step. Most of this is on you. Taking this step might be a bit frightening. But it should also be exciting. So let's get to it.

The evolution and mastery of your skills

The five skills that you need to learn and master on your journey into the Quantum Age are:

- IT financial management
- Critical thinking and analytical skills
- Communications and marketing
- Innovation and collaboration
- Leadership.

These skills are the building blocks that you will need going forward. They are highly interrelated and do not necessarily function in the form of a hierarchy. This means that you do not need to develop them in order. You can start anyplace that appeals to you. You can start with what you think may be easiest or hardest. You can try to develop gradually across all five of the skills, or you can pick one and put all of your focus there first. There is no one way to do it. There is no right way to do it. As long as you do it, you win.

That said, there are a few things that you should understand about them and the order in which they are presented above. If you are unsure of how or where to start, this order may help. The five skills are presented in a manner that represents a progression from more technical to more creative and from more concrete to more abstract. For most IT people, this progression may be the most comfortable. When you start with IT financial management, it may be an area that you are unfamiliar with, but it is still pretty straightforward. By the time you get to leadership, it starts to get much more abstract and conceptual. Again, there is no one way or right way, but you should think about how you will be most comfortable learning. Personally, I like a balanced approach, learning slowly on multiple fronts at once. That may or may not work for you. The most important thing is that you first begin, and then continue. Do it in whatever way will help you get going and stay on this journey.

Have you decided how you will begin? Have you started? If you haven't, then stop here and continue reading once you have somehow, someway, begun the learning process. Take your time. I'll wait.

OK, good. You have made the commitment to start the process of learning new skills. You have taken your first steps. I wanted to make sure that you were under way before I told you this next part. I did not want you to have second thoughts, because this is so important to your future. But now that you are under way, there is something that you need to know:

This process will never be completed.

Sorry, I know that I probably should have told you this before I let you get going. But we IT people like things with clear beginnings and ends. We don't like things that are open-ended and never-ending. So I was afraid that you might just gloss over this and never do anything if I told you up front. I hope you can forgive me.

The process of learning these new skills will never end. There is no certification program. You cannot get your 'foundation certificate' in IT Leadership or IT Communication and Marketing. I mean, I'm sure that someone will create one if they haven't already, but don't be fooled. The kind of real-world skill learning that we are talking about is a journey that does not end. You will never be finished. You will simply continue to evolve and improve your skills.

It really isn't much different from your technical skills in that regard. Are you still using the technical skills that you learned ten years ago? How about two years ago? They are still there, of course. They are part of the foundation. The historical record. The institutional knowledge. But if you tried to rely solely on the knowledge and skills you had ten or even two years ago, if you had never learned anything new, you would be dead in the water. This is really no different. This process of learning these new skills is not a temporary detour that you must take until you get back to the main road. This is a new way of operating. A new way of life.

As we look at the learning of these new skills as a continuing process, we stop looking for an end and instead begin to seek mastery. If that sounds a bit confusing to you, you're not alone. Many people confuse the term 'mastery' with this idea of being done with something. You have 'mastered' it. You have reached the pinnacle. You have learned all that there is to know. Done. You are now the master.

But mastery is really a process. The idea of mastery is founded on the foundational concept that you can never achieve complete excellence, that there is always something more to learn, that there is always a way to improve. Think of anyone you might consider a master either from history or in contemporary times. Leonardo da Vinci, Monet, Mozart, Yo-Yo Ma, Roger Federer, Jack Nicklaus, Michael Jordan – do you believe for one moment that any one of these great masters ever stopped trying to improve? Do you believe that they ever felt that they were good enough?

Evolution and mastery go hand in hand. In *The Fifth Discipline*, Senge identifies 'Personal Mastery' as one of the five disciplines that create a learning organization. He states:

Personal mastery is the discipline of continually clarifying and deepening our personal vision, of focusing our energies, of developing patience, and of seeing reality objectively. As such, it is an essential cornerstone of the learning organization – the learning organization's spiritual foundation.

Only by recognizing your learning process as an evolutionary one that seeks mastery will you have the right mindset. It is this view and understanding that will enable you to persevere and continue. You must see it as a journey. But it is also a journey that will offer a significant amount of personal fulfillment.

In his book *Drive*, Daniel Pink argues that personal mastery is one of the three primary elements of intrinsic motivation and a great source of personal satisfaction in life. He says:

Engagement as a route to mastery is a powerful force in our personal lives. While complying can be an effective strategy for physical survival, it's a lousy one for personal fulfillment. Living a satisfying life requires more than simply meeting the demands of those in control. Yet in our offices and our classrooms we have way too much compliance and way too little engagement. The former might get you through the day, but only the latter will get you through the night.

By entering this process with a recognition that you are beginning a journey that will never end, you will also be paving the way to a great source of fulfillment in your own life. If you see this as merely a chore, as just what you must do to be able to keep a job, well, frankly you shouldn't bother. It just will not work. You must see this for what it really is – a tremendous opportunity. A chance to take control of your career and your destiny as an IT professional. As you learn, evolve, and master these five skills, you will be setting yourself on a course in which you will certainly be able to do all that is required in the Quantum Age.

But, more importantly, I believe, you will be setting yourself on a course in which you can do anything.

IT financial management skills

Money is the language of business. Just not in IT.

In most IT organizations financial management has been reduced to annual budget exercises that are about as far removed from reality as you can imagine. While Total Cost of Ownership (TCO) and Return on Investment (ROI) statements are a fact of life in most large IT organizations today, the truth (even if no one wants to admit it) is that they are mostly works of fiction. It is not that we want to lie about the figures. Nor is it really that we don't care about the numbers – at least not exactly. It's just that for most of us the dollars and cents are an abstraction layer removed from our day-to-day reality. More than anything, this is a matter of our stance. We approach everything from a technical perspective rather than a business perspective. And this limits our ability to see the financial perspective clearly.

Almost every conversation in IT begins from one of a few perspectives: requirements, technology (as in refresh, updates, etc.), security, or some form of operational impact. Think of any conversation that you had recently that had to do with a new IT project. It was almost certainly discussed from one of these perspectives: 'We have a new set of requirements from the customer ...,' 'This [fill in the blank] is approaching end-of-life and will no longer be supported by the vendor, therefore we need to do an upgrade ...,' 'We have determined that we have a security risk that we must respond to, therefore ...,' or 'There has been a series of failures in our core, therefore we must ...'

The perspective is always technically driven in some sense. So when we come to the end of that discussion, we have a laundry list of whatever it is that we need to buy – and only then do we begin to contemplate the financial ramifications of the situation. The truth is, we wish we didn't have to. It actually annoys us most of the time. We've determined what needs to be done; why do we need an ROI statement?

Developing IT financial management skills really has two facets: understanding the logical constructs of financial management and learning how to apply them in the context of IT's business. Educating yourself on the fundamentals of finance is the easiest part of this equation. There are a multitude of resources available: everything from books specifically on IT financial management to community college courses on microeconomics. The bigger challenge is understanding how to apply these principles.

As a starting point, you must look at IT as a business – at least for the purposes of understanding how IT finance should work. As you educate yourself on the mechanics of general financial management principles, looking at the services that IT provides as the services of a business to its customers will help reduce the level of abstraction and make it more real for you. It is also the most helpful paradigm when attempting to understand how to apply the principles of financial management to IT.

Imagine that you owned a business producing and selling T-shirts. Your chief T-shirt designer comes to you and says that he needs $10,000 for a new machine that prints designs on T-shirts. How would you evaluate that purchase decision? Would you simply accept that, because he says it's needed, you should do it? Probably not. What is the first question you might ask? From what perspective would you look at this decision?

The first thing that any business owner is going to ask is the impact on sales, revenue, and profit. Will buying this new machine allow me to produce a new kind of product and thereby increase my sales? Will it allow me to produce more T-shirts with the same or fewer staff, thereby reducing costs and increasing profit? Will it produce T-shirts with fewer malfunctions thereby reducing my discards, reducing costs, and increasing profits? First off, if it's not going to have some kind of positive impact on your sales, revenue, or profits, the conversation will be over. Once it has cleared that hurdle, you will have in effect created an equation that will help you evaluate the decision. 'This $10,000 purchase will enable us to increase our profit by $1,000 per month.' With that understanding and perspective, you will be able to decide if it is worth the investment.

Notice that the first question had nothing to do with any technical aspect of the machine. It was purely financial as the first and primary perspective. Only after that determination had been made would the conversation progress into the technical realms. You may be thinking to yourself, 'But wait a minute. This isn't the same thing. This scenario is voluntary. You could choose not to do anything. When we are dealing with security or a system that is failing, we don't have that option. We have to do something.'

Really? Are you sure?

From a technical perspective, it may seem so. But it just is not the case from a business perspective. If you think about this on a personal level, you know that this is true. Is every single thing in your home in perfect working condition? (I'm sure that there are a few of you out there who will answer yes to this, but you are the exception!) For most of us, the answer is a resounding, 'Of course not.' In my case,

I have this garage door opener that opens perfectly, but takes a little finessing to get to close properly. Why have I let it go and not fixed it? Because the cost of repair will probably be $200 or $300 but the cost to me now is that I have to sit there and watch the door open and close numerous times before it gets closed 'just right.' For me, the cost is higher than the value of the fix. Someone else may value this differently, but, for me, I would rather invest my $200 somewhere else. At least for now. If it gets worse, if it gets more impactful, or if I just get tired of it, that may change. But for now, I'm OK.

That is a perfectly legitimate decision. But it can only be made from a financial perspective. I must start with looking at it in financial terms, because that is the only one that allows me to assess it from a value perspective. This is how your customer looks at nearly everything. So when we start with a technical perspective, we have completely left them behind.

Now, getting back to the IT-as-a-business paradigm, we can look at every single service that we provide as a product that we sell to our customers. Just like that T-shirt maker, every decision that we make can now be made from a financial perspective. Will this network upgrade allow me to increase my 'sales' (perhaps by improving the customer experience or enabling greater revenue for our customers) or reduce my cost of providing that service? You've probably recognized the biggest stumbling block to taking this approach – it requires that we have a price associated with every service and that we understand precisely what it costs us to deliver that service. That is basic information that every single business in America understands – but that your typical IT organization cannot even begin to guess at.

Developing your IT financial management skills involves changing two things: your financial acumen and your perspective on the role of finance in the day-to-day operations of all aspects of the business of IT. First, you need to teach yourself to become comfortable with numbers. No matter what your role may be, understand the cost and relative value of each transaction that you are involved in or support. Do not allow it to be 'someone else's problem.' You cannot afford to delegate or outsource it. If you do not own your own financial responsibility, you will not own your own destiny. Second, you need to flip everything around and put the product/service/financial perspective at the front and top of your operating paradigm. There should literally be essentially no conversation that does not begin from this perspective.

Learn to love numbers. Make them your friend. Learn to talk in terms of the products and services you provide, the value they deliver, and the cost components that are required to deliver it. Let that be the foundation for how you function and for how you make decisions. You will start to see things in a whole new light.

Critical thinking and analytical skills

Do you want to know the most evil phrase in all of IT? It is perhaps the single greatest destroyer of IT value in the last 10 years:

Best practices.

I remember talking to an IT executive during a particularly challenging consulting session. Getting tired and frustrated, he turned to me and said, "Charlie, can't you just tell me how everyone else does this and we'll just do the same thing?"

If I had a dollar for every time someone asked if I could just tell them what the best practice was so that they could follow it, well, I would have a whole lot of dollars. Don't get me wrong. I am a huge fan of ITIL, COBIT, IT-CMF and a bunch of the other IT frameworks out there. This is not a slam on so-called best-practice frameworks at all. It makes perfect sense to figure out what has worked for others and use it as a starting point in your own efforts. That is how humankind has advanced itself for millennia. Frameworks such as ITIL have simply distilled and codified those practices to make the process easier.

But the frameworks are meant to be the beginning point, not the end. They are not, nor were they ever, intended simply to be taken and applied 'by the book.' It was always meant to be an 'adopt and adapt' approach, whereby you adopt the key principles of the framework and then adapt them to your specific organization, your objectives, and your culture. OK, I will get off my soapbox now, but I do believe that this desire to simply take a 'best practice' and apply it is reflective of a larger challenge in IT organizations – in many ways, we fail to apply deep critical thinking and analytical skills.

We see this across the board. It happens in management circles, in operational circles, in development circles, and in security circles. No matter what part of IT you work in, it exists there. In an effort to standardize and simplify, we have homogenized and removed any opportunity to create targeted value in the process. Admittedly, this is in no small part a reaction to the needless customization that IT organizations deployed across vast swaths of the technology landscape in the mistaken belief that they were different and special in ways that they simply were not. Nevertheless, the overreaction toward simply adopting 'best practices' and 'out-of-the-box' solutions has robbed IT of one of its critical roles – applying critical thinking and analytical skills to ensure that technology investments provide the greatest return.

I remember sitting in a meeting with a Fortune 500 company during the early planning stages of a very large application rollout. And they trotted out the mantra – no customization. I pulled one of the executives aside and told him that I felt it was huge mistake. That it would unnecessarily restrict the very smart people in IT that they were paying a lot of money to be smart. They did not listen. Not surprisingly, the deployment of that very important system did not go very well.

Regardless of how we got here, as IT professionals we must reclaim this role. We are (typically) paid very well for the unique skills that we are supposed to bring to our organizations. We cannot therefore allow those skills to be reduced to the modern-day equivalent of factory work. If we are not allowed – or if we do not choose – to employ critical thinking and analytical skills in our day-to-day functions, then how much value can we really provide?

We simply cannot accept mantras like 'adopt best practices by the book' or 'no customization; implement it out of the box.' The problems that we are trying to solve and the solutions that they will entail are just not that simple. Now, this is not license to go back to the way things were. That is what got us into this mess to begin with. And I will argue that the reason that this happened in the first place is that we were not applying critical thinking and analytical skills to begin with. Had we been doing so, we would not have seen these crazy, nonsense customizations ever implemented.

So, what does it mean to develop, evolve, and master your critical thinking and analytical skills? Mostly, it just means that you need to think. But this is not about just applying some intellect. It is about applying context and judgment. Being analytical and applying critical thinking means that you are looking at the whole picture – not just the technical aspects of something. It means that you challenge assumptions, that you do not accept something at face value, and that you look at it in the context of your specific situation. Perhaps the simplest way of thinking about it can be summed up in a single word: *why?*

If you can get in the habit of always asking that question, *why?*, you will be taking a huge step forward. I am always amazed at how often that simple question can stump someone. During consulting engagements I will have someone walk me through a process. At some point, I will point to a step in the process and simply ask them why they are doing it. They will give me a 'what are you? Stupid?' look and say, 'Because that is what ITIL says.' To which I will respond, 'OK, so why does it apply to you in this situation?'

The blank looks are always priceless. Because the book said so. That was all they needed. Do not let that be you. Do not let that ever be enough. Always, always, ask why. Learning to challenge assumptions, learning to unabashedly ask why of everything, learning to look at everything in the context of your specific situation – these are what you need to learn to develop (and rekindle) your critical thinking and analytical skills. They are critical skills that are vitally important to building a learning and disciplined organization. And as you point the *why* outside the organization, they will help you to develop intimacy and create a truly dynamic organization.

Communication and marketing skills

Have you ever walked onto a used-car lot for whatever reason and thought to yourself, 'I am sure glad that I don't have this job.' Especially for those of us in IT, sales is often at or near the bottom of the list of what we like to do. I mean, there is a reason why we got into IT, right? And it was not because we enjoyed sales and marketing.

I've got some bad news for you. Whether you like it or not, you *are* in sales and marketing. Every day, you have a very important job to do. You need to communicate with your customers (whether they are internal to IT, elsewhere in the organization, or external to the organization) the importance and value of the service that you are providing. Every day. It is happening right now, you just may not realize it. With every single meeting, conversation, or interaction you have, people are assessing the value you bring to your relationship with them. It's kind of like there is a little stock-ticker in their head that ticks up or down like a stock market index based on their experience with you.

You do it too. It may be subconscious, but you are making the exact same kind of assessments and judgments of others based on how they work with you and treat you. Pause right here. Think of the three people who do the best work in your organization – the people you most enjoy working with. Now think of the three people who you just do not trust to get it done. First, I am pretty confident that you didn't have any trouble coming up with either of those lists. In fact, names probably just popped into your head as you read the words. There was probably not much thinking or contemplating involved. Now, think for a moment about why they popped into your head. How much of it was because of the actual product or service they delivered to you? That was probably some of it. But how much of it was because of how you *feel* when you work with them? How much of it is based on how they interact with you, how they relate with you?

In their simplest form, that is what communication and marketing skills are all about. They are about framing, shaping, and managing the experience we have with our customers. IT people sometimes have a difficult time understanding this. We tend to believe that our results should speak for themselves. That others will judge us solely based on our performance. In fact, we kind of find the idea that we have to market ourselves in any way somewhat insulting. 'If you're good at what you do, you don't need to spout off about it. People will know,' we think to ourselves. Unfortunately, it is just not true. We all make assessments on the performance of people, organizations, even entire countries, based on how we feel about our experience with them – even when the actual results may be inferior to the results that we get from someone else.

In the end, it comes down to our relationship. If the relationship is good, the experience will be good. And if the experience is good, their perception of us – and the value we offer – will be good. Our marketing and communication skills are one of the key ways in which we build, support, and maintain that relationship.

11: Five Skills

While I was working at the healthcare company in the early 1990s, it became very clear that we had a significant problem. Through a combination of growing pains and some inherited mess, we were suffering from some broad instability across several of our key systems. We had a pretty good handle on what was going on and we knew that it was going to take some time to fix. We were collecting both formal and informal satisfaction data at the time and it was clear that we were taking a hit. People were not happy and if we were right about the source of our problems, they were not going to be happy for a while.

So we put a special process in place. We identified all key executive stakeholders in the company and assigned each of them to one of our senior service desk agents. We gave each of our assigned service desk agents a strict protocol to follow: in the event of a service impact, they were to drop whatever they were doing and immediately place a call to their assigned executive. Even if we had no idea what was going on, we wanted them to hear about the impact first from us. They would then agree and commit to a specific follow-up protocol with their assigned executive. In some cases, they wanted to hear from us every five minutes. We agreed to provide them an update at whatever intervals they requested. Even if we had no further information to give them, they were going to get a call.

As I said, we had plenty of problems during that time, so our assigned service desk agents got to know their assigned executive fairly well. It was really not a great situation. But an amazing thing happened. Long before we were able to actually fix anything, our satisfaction numbers almost immediately shot up. And it was not just the executives; it was from all levels of the organization. The reason was fairly simple. People could accept that something had gone wrong. What they hated was having no idea what it was or what was being done about it. They hated being in the dark. Simply communicating with them, consistently and in a predictable manner – even when we had little information to share – went a long way to improving the customer experience. And when their staff called them to let them know that the systems were down again, they were not surprised. They were able to tell them that they were aware of the situation and that they understood what was being done to correct it. Therefore, their staff calmed down and the whole situation became manageable.

Eventually, we extended this protocol to deeper levels of the organization. Oh, and we did eventually get those problems ironed out. But our satisfaction problems had been resolved long before the technical solution had been put in place – solely based on our communication and marketing strategies.

It is absolutely impossible to overstate the importance of learning communication and marketing skills. It goes far beyond just managing expectations around problems, as in the example I just shared. It is also a key tool in your effort to change the attitudes and behaviors of your team and coworkers. As we work to transform ourselves, our teams, and our organizations, the way that we communicate and interact becomes vitally important. This can be difficult for IT people because it comes from the other side of the brain, but it is imperative that these skills be developed. Developing these skills means developing your creativity, becoming more empathetic (so that you can see things from others' perspective) and understanding that you cannot communicate and interact with everyone in the same way. You must learn to anticipate how people will react to information, to discern how they see value in relationships and interactions, and to discover how they are motivated.

We are getting into the harder part of your learning journey. These are skills that may come less freely to you. But they are worth the investment. A great place to start is with two books: *Switch* by Dan and Chip Heath and *Drive* by Daniel Pink. But however you get there, develop, evolve, and master these skills. They will have a huge impact across all five of the organizational traits.

Innovation and collaboration skills

I have already spent a lot of time on 'innovation.' How, as an industry, we started with great innovation. How we forgot to be innovative. Why we need to be innovative in order to become a dynamic organization. But virtually the entire discussion has been in an organizational context. If you think about it, we tend to think about innovation in this way. We speak of innovative organizations or innovative teams or even innovative periods. But when was the last time you described someone as innovative?

Why do you think this is?

Mostly, it is because the term 'innovation' implies collaboration. When we think of a lone, creative thinker, carving out some new space in the dark recesses of his basement, we think in terms of an inventor. Invention seems to be a solitary act, whereas innovation seems to invoke the idea of a social context. This is not strictly true from a perspective of the 'meaning of the word,' but it is how most of us associate the two words.

In the recent book *The Innovator's DNA*, by professors Jeff Dyer, Hal Gregersen, and Clayton Christensen, the authors identify five 'discovery skills' which they call the DNA that enables innovators to look at things differently: Associating, Questioning, Observing, Experimenting and Networking. In their view, the process notably begins and ends with elements of collaboration. The authors describe what is called the 'Medici effect,' coined by author Frans Johanssen. They explain that this refers to the:

creative explosion in Florence when the Medici family brought together creators from a wide range of disciplines – sculptors, scientist, poets, philosophers, painters, and architects. As these individuals connected, they created new ideas at the intersection of their respective fields, thereby spawning the Renaissance, one of the most innovative eras in history.

The idea at the beginning of the innovation process is to expand beyond your own perspectives, expose yourself to a broad range of ideas and then allow your mind to freely associate these seemingly disparate ideas into something new. At the end of the process (and throughout), the authors identified that great innovators do what they call "networking." They don't simply take their idea, develop it and call it done. Instead, they share it with others from a wide range of disciplines and who have a wide range of perspectives. Great innovators, the authors found, are not protective. They explore and share freely with a wide range of people to expand their knowledge and their perspectives, regardless of how finished the idea may be. In fact, throughout all five of the identified 'discovery skills,' innovators are consistently interacting with others through their observations, questioning, and experimentation.

This stands in great contrast to how we typically think of great innovation. We have this idea that there are these flashes of great insight, which you then run off and develop into something great. While that is often the case, it doesn't just happen. It comes at the end of a long process that is largely social in nature. Most importantly, the authors point out, is that it is driven as much by a discipline of these specific behaviors – these 'discovery skills' – and that means that they can be learned and developed.

When we talk about innovation within the context of IT, there are really two kinds: technology innovation and process innovation. As we move from a manufacturing to a retail operating paradigm, most true technology innovation will come from outside the organization. Technology providers, whose entire existence is built around developing new technologies, will have far greater resources to create broad-based technology-driven innovations. That does not mean that IT organizations and IT professionals within them cannot create technology innovations, but it will be much less common. On the other hand, there is a tremendous opportunity to engage in process innovation within IT organizations.

Process innovation is not about implementing the latest ITIL or COBIT process. It is the ability to see things in a different light and to be able to take existing elements and put them together in a new way that creates significantly more value for the organization. If we apply the five discovery skills presented in *The Innovator's DNA*, how many opportunities are there within our IT organizations to leverage technology in ways that will create surprising and unexpected results? I believe that there is a wealth of opportunity lying beneath our feet if we can only see it for what it is.

In the early 1920s, my great-grandparents moved from New Mexico to California to start a new life. They bought a piece of land near the top of a hill with the intent to farm it and raise small livestock. After a short time, they sold the land because they found it to be infertile. It was a great disappointment. The reason why the land was infertile was because there was too much of this "black, sticky stuff everywhere," as my grandmother would say. So they moved on. That land turned out to be one of the richest oil fields in Southern California. But my great-grandparents did not understand the opportunity that lay beneath their feet, so they moved on, leaving this 'infertile' ground to others to harvest in another way.

This is the situation that you find yourself in. You are standing on a vast oil field of opportunity if you can only see it for what it is. You may find it to be 'infertile,' frustrated by the politics and the infighting. But if you can apply the five discovery skills, you will find the vast opportunities that lie just beneath the surface.

To do this, there are some key points that you should take away. First is that the foundation of this process is to create new associations from seemingly unrelated ideas. You need to create your own 'Medici effect.' Get into the habit of expanding beyond your own circle – in terms of both industry and technical domain. Attend seminars and conferences that are far outside your normal domains. Convene lunches with people from around IT and from around the company to simply explore ideas and areas of interest. It almost doesn't matter which topics you discuss – the act of exploring ideas will give your mind the freedom to create associations of these kinds and identify new areas to explore.

You need to also get in the habit of observing and questioning. It will likely take some effort. In many ways, we are programmed to have answers, not questions. You need to learn to observe without bias. Spend time with your customers simply watching how they utilize technology – in what ways are they using it in unexpected ways? But you must be cautious not to get trapped. Your job in this process is not to look for answers, to find incremental improvements, or to identify defects in the software. Your goal is to use these observations to see things differently. To discover unexpected ways in which technology can be applied to solve problems – perhaps problems that the customer has not yet even identified. Part of this process is to develop the skill of questioning. You must learn to question everything. Hold nothing sacred. Learn to look at things without constraint. 'In a perfect world, if I had no limits placed upon me, if no investments had been made, how might I approach this problem differently?'

These skills will serve as the foundation for innovation. They will create a 'free-flowing' mindset that will allow you to see things differently. But the world of IT is complex and it will be rare that you will be able to see things broadly enough on your own to create breakthrough innovations. This is where the skills of experimentation and networking will come into play. In the Quantum Age, no IT organization will stand alone. Virtually every service you provide will be delivered through a complex supply chain that will extend far beyond the walls of your IT organization. So don't believe for a moment that you will be able to create breakthrough innovations on your own. You must get comfortable engaging your suppliers, your partners, and your customers as part of the innovation process. You must let go of the idea that you are only there to 'get requirements' or 'give requirements.' You need to give yourself the freedom to go into a meeting without answers or commands – and be comfortable simply having the questions.

By creating this kind of 'network' and engaging its members consistently, you will discover new and powerful ideas. Most importantly, these ideas will not be bound by the constraints of your organization's internal capabilities. But you must recognize that this will be a bit like being a baseball player. If you bat .300, meaning that only 30% of your ideas prove valuable, you will be a wild success! You must get comfortable with failure. But you must also learn to 'fail fast.' This is where the idea of experimentation comes in. Learning to test out your ideas early in the cycle, long before they are 'ready' and within the broad platform of your network, will enable you to evolve and improve your ideas rapidly.

There is a desperate need in IT organizations for this kind of innovation leadership. IT professionals who can build these networks; create new and interesting associations; and facilitate the process of questioning, observing, and experimenting will become some of the most valuable people in the organization. They will also be having the most fun.

The good news is that these are skills that you can develop. Being an innovation and collaboration leader is simply a choice.

Leadership skills

What does it mean to be a leader?

The idea of leadership may be one of the most heavily covered topics in business. It is an idea that is at once commonly understood and abstract. As humans, we have a great need for leadership. We want, we need, there to be a leader in almost every situation. Yet, too often, particularly in our corporate lives today, it is just as likely that no one will be willing to stand up, to put themselves out there, and be a leader. The risks, it seems, are too great. The reward too small. But this causes a vacuum, often with disastrous results.

In 2009, Air France Flight 447 left from Rio de Janeiro bound for Paris. A few hours into the flight, it disappeared. Five days later, the wreckage was found. All 228 passengers and crew had been lost. The plane, an Airbus A330, is one of the most technologically advanced airplanes ever built, so this crash became a great mystery in the world of avionics. It took an extraordinary effort (and bordered on a miracle), but eventually the flight recorder was found in 12,000 feet of water. The story it told was harrowing and, in my opinion, showed the horrible effects that can result from a leadership vacuum.

On that fateful night, the flight was headed into a strong Atlantic storm. Unfortunately, they were not able to see the severity of a second storm system immediately behind the one they were headed into. Because it seemed to be business as usual, the captain went to the rear of the plane to take a nap. After he was gone, everything started to go wrong. Losing a series of key sensors, the two first officers had to take control of the plane by hand. The severity of the storm put them both into a panic and because neither of them was clearly in charge, they inadvertently ended up fighting for control of the airplane. The series of decisions and actions they took that night within this vacuum of leadership eventually resulted in the plane stalling and then crashing into the sea.

Lack of leadership almost always leads to bad outcomes. But leadership is not management. Most of us are guilty of seeing them as one and the same. Yet, having top management lack leadership skills has become all too common in IT organizations. At the same time, some of the most successful efforts are successful because of strong leadership (even if we don't recognize it that way) from deep within the organization – not from top management. As we move into the Quantum Age, we can no longer afford to ignore and hope. We must recognize that effective leadership skills will be mandatory in this time of great change. And we must acknowledge that strong leadership skills will be required at all levels of the organization. There will be no room for anyone who does not see themselves as an IT leader and act accordingly.

But what does it mean to build and develop leadership skills? What does that look like in an IT context?

I believe that, first and foremost, it means being willing to accept it as your personal duty not to accept the status quo any longer – to stand up and lead change wherever and whenever you see that change is required. Being an IT leader in the Quantum Age will require that you no longer wait for those 'on top' to decide what must be done and then simply 'do your job.' It means being an active participant and a willing accomplice. And if you are the person 'on top,' you must recognize that you cannot, and should not, do it all alone. Leadership must occur at all levels, because change will be required at all levels.

A simple, yet extremely concise, recipe for what it means to be this type of leader was written over 2,000 years ago. In *The Art of War*, Sun Tzu identifies the five virtues of leadership: wisdom, trustworthiness, benevolence, courage, and discipline. While this obviously has application far beyond the world of IT, it is an extremely helpful context as you seek to develop the specific leadership skills that you will need in this new era of IT.

Wisdom

In our context, this may be best translated as applying good judgment. This is relevant in two ways. First, in accepting your duty that you must stand up to lead change, you must apply good judgment in determining what it is that should be changed. This is not about simply instituting change for the sake of change. It will take the wisdom of your experience to challenge everything – including your own history, bias, and misconception. Second, you must also apply judgment in how you execute those changes. Try to tackle too much and your efforts will go down in a blaze of glory. Too little and you will have no impact. The key to leading this change will be to diligently apply effective judgment in everything you do.

Trustworthiness

Your effective application of judgment and the demonstration of your wisdom will be an important element in developing the second virtue, trustworthiness. Simply stated, no one will follow someone whom they do not trust. This trust is personal. This is about your personal and individual relationship with others. Do you say it like it is? Do you do what you say? Do people believe you when you tell them something? This can be tough because we all view ourselves as trustworthy. Ask for the honest opinion of people around you. Do your actions convey the trustworthiness you seek to project? Leadership in the Quantum Age will not be about position. Rarely will anyone *have* to follow you. Instead, you must inspire them to follow you. It will start with your demonstration of wisdom, but it will be sealed by whether or not they believe you and trust in you.

Benevolence

This is not a word that is used too often any longer, particularly in the context of leadership. We tend to have this image of the strong leader, facing the onslaught, fearlessly leading his troops into battle. But Sun Tzu is pointing out a universal truth that we sometimes forget. The greatest leaders in our lives are always those who, we believe, care about us the most. The fact that someone cares about us, our needs, and our well-being makes us much more willing to follow them. Even when someone has a great vision about doing something that you know is important, when you feel that they only care about themselves, you will hesitate to get involved. As you step out to lead in the Quantum Age, you must demonstrate to all of those around you that you sincerely care about them. You must put their interests above yours in the quest to achieve something bigger than either of you.

Courage

We have discussed courage already, but it is important that you see this on a personal level. The sign of true leadership is someone who has the courage to step forward, despite their fear and regardless of who is or is not following them, to do what they know to be right. Challenging the status quo is not easy. As we move into the Quantum Age, there will be many who are afraid of the changes occurring. They will resist and they will fight to keep things as they are and have always been. Many of these people will be in senior management positions. It will take equal amounts of wisdom (to know when and where to make your stand) and courage (to do it) to overcome this inertia. Your willingness to be courageous in spite of the challenges and your fears will inspire further trust – from others and in yourself.

Discipline

Discipline is one of the five organizational traits, but it is also an important personal trait. In terms of leading yourself and others into the Quantum Age, it really means two things. First, it means having the fortitude to stick with it. Courage will be what is required to take the first few steps, but it is discipline that will keep you going. As you question and challenge, as you inspire others to follow, there will be a continued (if often subtle) effort to undermine your efforts. Whether they are conscious or subconscious, those with the most invested in the way things have always been will fight to keep it that way. It will only be through extraordinary personal discipline that you will be able to stay the course. Discipline also means one other thing – remaining true to your principles. With whatever change you seek to make, there will be two strategies employed to fight the change. One will be outright resistance. But the other is more insidious. Those opposed to the change will seem to agree to it and then slowly chip away at it until they have effectively neutered it. Compromise is good. It is a key part of getting things done. But if you compromise on your key principles then your efforts will be lost. To lead effectively in the Quantum Age you must be acutely aware of those principles which must be held steadfast, and then you must have the discipline to hold them.

Embracing the change and preparing for your future

At this point, you could be either incredibly excited or you could be shaking your head trying to figure out what you're going to do. On the one hand, these five skills are nothing new. It will be easy to gloss over them and think to yourself, 'This was a waste. I already have all of these skills.' But if you are honest with yourself, you know that you have plenty of room to grow and develop in each of these areas. We all do. The degree to which you accept this and then actively and diligently endeavor to improve yourself in each of these areas is what will make all of the difference to your future.

As I hope has been made clear, this change is coming. The world of IT as we know it is changing. It is bigger than any one of us. It is being driven by forces that are outside our direct control. But this does not mean you are hopeless or helpless. You must accept that you cannot stop this change from coming. But you must also accept that your future, your destiny, is in your hands. You can succeed and thrive during this change. You can play a key role in making it a reality. You can help lead your team and those around you into this era.

All it takes is a choice.

You simply must choose to believe this is happening. Believe that it is within your power to develop these skills and change your future. And then you must choose to act.

You must choose to learn. You must choose to practice and evolve your skills. And you must choose to start now.

Chapter 11 key points

Every IT professional needs to master five new skills – the skills of the Quantum Age IT organization – to thrive in the future. These are less technical skills and more business skills. They are: IT financial management, critical thinking and analytical skills, communications and marketing skills, innovation and collaboration skills, and leadership skills.

Here are the key points you should remember from this chapter:

- These five skills are not a hierarchy – you can develop them in any way that appeals to you.

- The process of learning these new skills will never end. You will simply continue to evolve and improve your skills.

- The goal is to seek mastery – to continually seek excellence.

- To understand effective financial management, we must begin by looking at IT as a business.

- You must learn to love numbers and to talk in terms of the products and services you provide, the value they deliver, and the cost components that are required to deliver them.

- 'Best practices' is an evil phrase if it causes us to simply accept something 'out of the box' and not think critically about what we are trying to accomplish.

- You need to get in the habit of always asking the question, 'Why?'

- Every person in IT is in sales and marketing. Every day you must communicate to your customers the value of the services that you are providing to them.
- In their simplest form, marketing and communication skills are about framing, shaping, and managing the customer experience.
- Innovation requires that you expand beyond your own perspectives, expose yourself to a broad range of ideas, and then allow your mind to freely associate these seemingly disparate ideas into something new.
- There are two types of innovation: technology and process innovation. In most IT organizations, the vast majority of innovation will be process innovation.
- You must get comfortable engaging your suppliers, your partners, and your customers as part of the innovation process.
- Leadership is not management.
- *Every* IT professional should see themselves as an IT leader and act accordingly.
- Being an IT leader in the Quantum Age will require that you no longer wait for those 'on top' to decide what must be done and then simply 'do your job.' It will mean being an active participant and a willing accomplice.
- IT leaders should be: Wise, Trustworthy, Benevolent, Courageous, and Disciplined.

CHAPTER 12: YOUR ROAD AHEAD

In 1492, Christopher Columbus left Spain in search of a westerly route to Asia.

In 1927, Charles Lindbergh boarded his plane at Roosevelt Field near New York City heading to Paris France on what he hoped would be the first solo transatlantic flight.

On July 16, 1969, Neil Armstrong sat in the capsule of Apollo 11 preparing to blast off on the first manned mission to the Moon.

Thus began three of the greatest expeditions, three of the greatest adventures, of all time. But, of course, this was not really the beginning of any of these. Each of them had started first with a simple decision. A decision that a step forward would be taken. And while each journey is now synonymous with a single person, each of them involved hundreds of people to make the expedition a success.

I don't know if your journey into the Quantum Age will enter the annals of history as one of its great intellectual expeditions. I expect that it probably will not. But I do know that it will share many of the attributes of these great expeditions. It will begin with a single decision. Yours. It will require a deep commitment and a willingness to sacrifice for what you believe in – for what you know can be. And it will not be something that you do on your own.

Your road ahead may not be a great expedition of the order of those of Columbus, Lindbergh, or Armstrong. But it will be one of your great journeys. If you choose to accept the challenge and set out on this journey, you will remember this moment. You will forever remember it as the moment when you chose to take control of your own destiny and lead yourself and those around you into your future.

One person at a time

The first three sections of this book deal with things at the organizational level. How the function of IT was created. How organizations lost their way. The looming threat to organizations. And the five organizational traits that IT teams need to develop.

But for all of the discussion about organizations, this final section of the book showed that the engine for all of this change is an individual.

It is you.

As an industry, we will only be able to make the transition into the Quantum Age successfully if you (and thousands of others just like you) make the decision to do it. Whether you are an IT executive or just starting out, the situation is the same. You must choose to be a part of the solution. You must choose to be a part of the future. You must choose to learn, develop, and evolve the new skills and to help your organization adopt the five traits.

The transition to the Quantum Age will not happen in some big blast. It will not happen in some big organizational transformation trumpeted from on high. It will only happen one way.

One person at a time.

As the previous two chapters hopefully made clear, this can only happen if you step up, embrace the coming change, and develop these five skills. They are the building blocks that every organization will need in the future. As this transition becomes more and more obvious, these skills will be in high demand. So, yes, learning and developing these skills is good for your career. But it is also critical to the future of our entire industry. We simply cannot afford to wait until everyone is 'on board.' We cannot wait and try to do this all together as one big group. Some of you, frankly, will not get it. I am sorry, but we cannot wait for you. Those who see it, who understand it, must and will act now.

One person at a time.

That is how the Quantum Age will arrive. As has been true of almost every other major change we have seen, there is no trumpeted announcement. There is no global declaration. But, slowly and steadily, a small group of people see the need and opportunity for change and step up to take it. By the time the majority of people understand that something is happening, it has already happened. We are at that beginning. And we are counting on you to join us.

A personal journey, but not alone

No one can make this decision for you. One person at a time means that every person must make this choice on their own. But while this is a personal journey, you are not alone. The decision to begin must be personal. You must want to change. You must want to be part of the solution, part of the future. Even if everyone else around you is getting on board, you cannot simply 'jump on the bandwagon.' It just will not work. You have to believe. You have to want it.

But once that decision is made, once you begin the process, something will become very clear. Not only do you not have to do it alone – you cannot do it alone. Virtually every element of both the five skills and the five traits involves other people. Whether it is your coworkers, your suppliers, or your customers, everything revolves around a social dialogue. This transition into the Quantum Age is social.

While it is clear that social technologies will have a transformative impact both on how IT operates and on the services it provides, the real catalyst for change will not be the social technology, but rather the purely human social interactions that must occur. As you and others develop these five skills, the fundamental social makeup of yourself, and therefore of the organization, will begin to change. You will have the tools personally and structurally to engage in meaningful and consistent conversations with your customers, suppliers, and fellow IT professionals. And those discussions will change everything.

For Mother's Day this year, I gave my wife a gift that is very scary for me – dance lessons. You see, my wife loves to dance. At least in theory. The problem is that neither of us are very good at it. We just never had a great reason to learn, nor much opportunity to practice it. If we are at a wedding or other event and everyone is out there dancing around, then no problem. We'll go. But if no one has ventured onto the floor yet, well, there is just no way that you are going to get me out there. The last thing in the world that I want is to let the whole world know that I cannot really dance. So, we sit there and wait until enough people have begun dancing to convince ourselves that no one will notice us. Unfortunately, a lot of times that point never comes. So we just sit there. Wanting to dance, but afraid of being the fool.

The single greatest risk or fear about something like the ideas in this book is that no one wants to be first. Everyone is afraid of looking foolish. Afraid of looking like they don't know what they are doing. But the situation is different from my dance challenges. Because you are not alone. When you take that first step out there, you will not be all alone on a dance floor. Instead, you will be joining a conga line, engaging with people as you develop your skills and embed the five traits into your organization.

Assemble your tribe

In his landmark book *Tribes*, Seth Godin describes a tribe as simply "a group of people connected to one another, connected to a leader, and connected to an idea." His basic position is that in this new digital era, anyone can start a movement. It takes no more than an idea and a willingness to lead. We all want to be part of a tribe. We need to be a part of a tribe. We want to believe in something bigger than ourselves. We want to do something that is important, meaningful.

For those of us in IT, I completely believe that this is that chance. In ways big and small, local and global, each and every one of us has the opportunity to create our own Quantum Age movement. Wherever you are right now, that is where your movement can begin. But, in case you have not gotten the message, you cannot do it alone. So assemble your tribe.

Go out into your world and talk about these ideas. Talk about the changes that are occurring. Don't just talk about the stories and examples in this book. Apply it to your real world. Can you see the threat? Can you see the changes happening? Do those around you see it? Share it, discuss it, and begin creating momentum for change. Share the idea, be the leader, and build your tribe around you. If you are excited about what you have read, they will be too. If you believe that the threat is real, that opportunity exists, and that you can be an agent of change, then they will believe it of you as well, and of themselves.

Within whatever organization you call home, I can promise you one thing – there are other people just like you somewhere in the organization. The fact that you have read this far, that you are still reading, means that you are different. It means that you get it. And it means that you really do want to do something about it. You are not alone. There are others. But, like you, they have learned that raising your hand is a great way to get it slapped. So they stay hidden in the shadows, waiting for an opportunity to come along to really make a difference.

Give them that opportunity.

Seek those people out and share your ideas with them. Share your beliefs with them. Share your faith that change is possible and that it must happen in your organization. If you have found the right people, they will nod. They will agree. They will be ready to be a part of the change. They are your tribe. Be their leader and make something happen.

Set off on your great adventure

When Christopher Columbus, Charles Lindbergh, and Neil Armstrong set off on their great explorations, success was far from certain. They didn't set out with any guarantees. They didn't set out with any promises of success. They didn't begin their journeys believing that they would be simple or easy. In fact, there were far more things that could go wrong than could go right.

But here is what they did have.

They had a vision for what they wanted to achieve. It wasn't mushy. It was crystal clear. They knew what they were doing, they knew why they were doing it, and they understood the risks involved. They had a vision – and eyes wide open.

They also had a team. Not one of these men, or the many other great men and women explorers through the ages, ever did anything truly big or momentous on their own. Lindbergh had the backing of nine investors and an entire aircraft company at his disposal. Christopher Columbus had a crew of 87 and three ships on his first journey. They knew that they were only as strong as the team they led.

Finally, they had a spirit of adventure. These were men who looked into the unknown not with fear, but with great anticipation. They looked into that unknown future and saw hope. They saw a vision of what could be. They enjoyed the adventure and spread that joy to their teams so that they could lead them on a journey whose destination was not fully known and whose outcome was far from certain.

As we stand at the precipice and look out upon our unknown future, we have the same opportunity. We can shrink from it and let it win. Or we can rise to the challenge with a sense of adventure. We are at the edge of a new era for IT organizations. We stand poised at the boundary between these two points in time. Our future is coming. Will you take that step and lead us on a great adventure into the Quantum Age?

RESOURCES FOR YOUR QUANTUM AGE JOURNEY

A PRACTICAL GUIDE TO GETTING STARTED

Hopefully, this book has accomplished two things: made it clear that the world of IT is changing and inspired you to be a part of leading that change forward.

That decision takes courage. It represents a willingness to accept that much of what you have known about how IT operates is going to change. And it means a willingness to let go of much of the comfort that comes with knowing how things are supposed to work. In return, you will get a lot of uncertainty. A lot of fear. A lot of doubt. But you will also have the opportunity to be a part of what I believe to be the most significant transition in the history of our young industry. I truly believe that this is going to be one of the most exciting and rewarding times to be an IT professional. Welcome to the journey.

Now that we are done patting ourselves on the back, we have some work to do. But where and how should you start? This section will give you some starting points – a few places to start your journey. Good luck. I am rooting for you!

Your reading list

Do you remember your first day in college? What is the first thing you got? That's right – a reading list. A list of books that you should read to prepare your mind for the term ahead. Well, I have one for you too and it is the best place to begin your journey.

Following is a list of books that I highly recommend you read. Many of these are the books that have been referenced in my writing, but I have also thrown in some others that round things out. What you will notice is that none of them are about IT. They deal with the fundamental issues of building the type of organization that we need to create in the Quantum Age. These qualities are universal and are not unique to IT. There is another thing that is important about this list and your own personal development. It is critical that you expand your reference points far beyond the world of IT. Many of the problems that we, as an industry, are facing have been faced by others. Many of those stories and those lessons can be found in these books. As the authors of *The Innovator's DNA* showed us, the ability to associate is critical to our ability to innovate and think beyond our bounds. Reading these books is a great way to begin that process.

Your recommended reading list

The Fifth Discipline, Peter Senge

Breaking the Fear Barrier, Tom Rieger

The Speed of Trust, Stephen M.R. Covey

Predictably Irrational, Daniel Ariely

What Got You Here Won't Get You There, Marshall Goldsmith

Drive, Daniel Pink

Linchpin, Seth Godin

Tribes, Seth Godin

Made to Stick, Dan and Chip Heath

Switch, Dan and Chip Heath

Tipping Point, Malcolm Gladwell

Blink, Malcolm Gladwell

Leading Change, John P. Kotter

The Innovator's DNA, Clayton Christensen, Jeff Dyer, and Hal Gregersen

The Discipline of Market Leaders, Michael Treacy and Fred Wiersema

Competitive Advantage, Michael Porter

Frameworks to guide you

One of the big takeaways from this book should also be that we can no longer accept the status quo or believe that things can continue as they always have been. We need fresh ideas and fresh perspectives to solve new and emerging problems. We need people who can apply critical thinking, innovation, and leadership skills to create new organizations from the old.

But that does not mean that we should do everything from scratch.

Rather than blowing up what we've built in the past, I think that it's better to view this as building a new city upon the foundation of an old one. Much of what we have done in the past will remain valid, it will just need to be adapted for our new circumstances. Particularly when it comes to core operational disciplines, we are foolish if we do not leverage the many frameworks that have been built by very smart people over long periods of time. They represent proven practices that, when used as tools (instead of one-size-fits-all instant answers), are extremely powerful aids in your march into the Quantum Age. You should use them as the foundation to building your learning, disciplined, and transparent organization.

Which framework?

I am sometimes asked which framework should be used or which is best. There is no right answer to this question. When I began writing this book, I was very curious as the 'right' number of words to qualify the work as an appropriate book. I found the best answer on a blog from a 'wise man' who said: "*As many as you need and not one more.*" It is the same with choosing which frameworks to use, if any. You should use exactly as many as you need and not one more. There are no brownie points for being the organization that adopts the most frameworks. They are merely tools and should be used to whatever degree they help you create the type of organization that you and your customers demand. It is also important to note that you may choose to use select elements from many of the frameworks. There is no right answer – they are just tools that are at your disposal.

Still, each of these frameworks has something to offer and is worth a look. At a minimum, you should review and evaluate each of these in the context of your goals and objectives. Where you find something of value, use it. Where you do not, move on.

Frameworks, methodologies and bodies of knowledge to consider:

ITIL

COBIT

IT-CMF

BiSL

PMBoK

Lean Six Sigma

CMMi/CMMi for Services

The Telemanagement Forum (TMF) NGOSS

Parallel paths

Once you have some reading under your belt and have examined some frameworks to guide you through the early stages, you are ready to get going. So, where do you start? With the skills that you need to develop? Or with the five organizational traits?

Yes!

That 'yes' is meant in two ways. First, to a certain degree, it doesn't matter. Just get started. Don't let this be one of those situations where you let a bunch of analysis get in your way. There is much to learn and much to do. Pick the path of least resistance and get started. There will be an abundance of barriers in your way. Find the path that is the least encumbered – and begin walking down it. If there is one of the five skills – or even a specific element of one of the skills – that speaks to you and in which you believe you can make a difference, then start there. If there is a political appetite to begin developing one of the five traits in your organization and you have an opportunity to be a part of it, then do it.

There is definitely a sense of order with both the five traits and the five skills, but you can literally begin moving forward in any area for some time before you'll hit any meaningful dependencies. The most important thing here is to create momentum and to find some early success. So, find and create the situation that is most likely to allow you to get moving.

That 'yes' was also meant in another way. You should feel free to begin work in multiple areas if that is helpful to you. Some people like to work linearly. Some have a bit more of an 'attention deficit disorder' personality and can never be happy doing only one thing at a time. If you want to begin with three skills and working on two traits, then do it. The same rule about getting started applies. The most important things are momentum and early success – especially if you are involving others. So make sure that you don't take on more than you can handle. You need to have a reasonable opportunity to be successful. But if you want to work on multiple areas at once, as long as it works for you, then do it.

The most important thing is simply to begin. If you start this process in earnest and commit to see it through for a period of time, you will build momentum, you will achieve success, and you will be on your way.

Your personal journey

Whichever order you choose, part of your journey will be personal. When you are building skills, it is essentially a personal activity. Some of the skills require more interaction than others, but all of them are essentially about *you* doing something. The difficult part is that there will be no one requiring you to do it. There is no shiny certificate at the end. In fact, many people may not even notice. It can be easy to get demoralized, to believe that the effort has no meaning, and to get distracted by more urgent (but probably less important) activities. As you begin your personal journey, you need to employ a strategy to protect yourself from these doubts and distractions.

To do so, there are five essential steps that you must take on your personal journey:

- Assess and Inventory
- Create Your Plan
- Set Your Targets
- Go Public
- Find an Accountability Partner.

Assess and inventory

The first step is to do a little introspection. You need to look at both where you have the greatest weaknesses and where you have the greatest interest and something to build upon. You should give yourself a good, hard look in each of the five skill areas. You are looking for the area that offers the greatest opportunity to find some quick, initial success. You need to build some momentum. You need to convince yourself that you can do it.

Go through each skill and give yourself a one-to-five rating in two categories: weakness/strength and disinterest/interest. This is not science, but this little tool will help you apply a more objective eye to your current skills. As you look at each of the five skills, ask yourself how strong or weak you are currently in the context of how they were presented. Then do the same in terms of how much that particular skill set interests you. Be honest with yourself. You are looking for those skill areas that interest you the most, but that are also your weakest. They will be the ones that you are most likely to start and stick with long enough to see some positive results. Once you have found some success, that will power you through those areas that are less interesting to you.

Create your plan

Once you know where you stand, lay out a simple plan. Identify the skill area or areas you are going to improve and then identify some of the specific attributes that you will work on. It may make sense to break it up so that you do not take on more than you can handle. You may start with one or two areas or components and then add something additional after two months or after you've reached some achievement level. Think through some specific actions that you can take to execute your plan. For instance, your plan may include specific behaviors like subscribing to an economics magazine and reading at least five articles from every issue, or perhaps reading at least three blog posts on leadership each week. Or maybe you will commit to going to one IT and one non-IT community function every month to expand your network. Frankly, it doesn't matter all that much what your plan says. Its importance is more in the process of putting a plan to paper. The mere act of doing it will cement it in your mind and make you much more committed to making something happen. So think about what you want to accomplish and what you want to improve. Then write it down.

Set your targets

A plan is important. But how will you know if you have achieved anything? To do that, you need to set some targets. With these skill areas, that might be hard to do, but if you have identified specific behaviors that you plan to model, then you should be able to monitor them. The goals you set are important. Too easy or completely detached from your plan and they will be worthless. Too hard or requiring too much work to monitor and you will give them up. Ensure that your goals are relevant and manageable. And don't worry if they're not perfect. You can always change or massage them. The important thing is to get something in place so that you can begin monitoring your progress. If you're measuring it, you will be much more likely to stick with it.

Go public

At this point, you are ready to get going. But as hard as it may be to get started, keeping it going will be even harder. The further removed you get from right now, the less urgent this will seem. It will be easy to get distracted, to forget why you are doing this and to begin wondering if this is all worth it. You need to be proactive to keep these road blocks from seeping into your consciousness. One of the easiest ways to do this is to go public with your intent. Put your plans in writing and publish them or share them somehow. Do not let this be your little secret. Tell people what you are doing. Post it on LinkedIn, Facebook, and Twitter. Tell people what you are doing and why. Once it's out there, you'll have created a powerful, self-reinforcing incentive to make it happen. I actually used this exact approach when writing this book. A little over a year ago, I posted on my blog and on twitter that I was going to write a book. Several people commented on it. From that point on, any time that I doubted, that I felt that maybe I should just drop this silly idea, my mind came back to the fact that I had told the world (at least the world that pays attention to me) that I was going to do this. Did I really want to be a flake and not deliver on my public promise? As evidenced by the fact that you are reading this, obviously the answer was no. This type of self-inflicted peer pressure can be a great tool to keep you on track.

Find an accountability partner

On a similar note, you need to find a confidant. Someone who you can share your plans and expectations with – and then ask them to hold you accountable. This is more than just confiding in a friend. You need an 'accountability partner.' You need someone who will see it as their duty to hold your feet to the fire. Set up a standing call or meeting with your accountability partner for the express purpose of reviewing your plans and what you are doing to realize them. They need to know that you *expect* them to be hard on you – and you need to be open and accept their questioning. A good accountability partner can keep you focused, keep you moving, and act as a personal coach and cheerleader. Let them. More than anything, at those times when you want to give up or when you just try to do the 'minimum,' they will help to keep you honest and keep you going.

Your organizational journey

When you are ready to begin your organizational journey, you need to recognize that you will be trying to fundamentally change the behaviors of people within your organization. Whether you are trying to get your small team of three to build a trait or trying to change a very large organization, the fundamental challenges will remain the same. Regardless of which organizational trait you are trying to instill, you will need to use the following six core building blocks:

- Give People a Reason to Change
- Create a Vision of What You Will Create
- Establish Clear, Measurable Objectives
- Define Specific Activities or Improvements that are Required to Realize the Objectives
- Communicate, Communicate, Communicate
- Rinse and Repeat.

Give people a reason to change

People are naturally resistant to change. We especially don't like being told that we have to change – or how we will have to change. So rather than try to drag folks along kicking and screaming, you need to offer them some very real reasons to change. You need to help them see the risks, the threats, and the opportunities. The biggest barrier is the illusion of safety in the status quo. You need to help them see that the status quo is, in fact, the riskiest and scariest place of all. No matter how much effort it takes, you need to stick with it until you have convinced people of the need to change. Until you have that, nothing else will matter.

Create a vision of what you will create

Once you have people on board that change is coming, the next question will be, 'Change into what?' Based on the principles and ideas in this book, you need to craft a vision of the type of organization that you want to create. Of course, you need to adapt this to the scope of the team that you are working with. There is no point in creating a vision that represents change for a 5,000-person organization, when you only have the ability to drive change in your four-person team. Scale the vision to your scope of influence, but ensure that it clearly articulates a statement of where you are going. Everyone should be able to see this vision clearly and what it will mean to the organization. Most importantly, they should be able to see themselves within this vision. One last note on the scope of the vision. If you feel strongly that the change needs to be bigger than the scope of your influence, that is OK. But it means that you are going to have to sell your vision to get the necessary support to get going.

Establish clear, measurable objectives

Have vision, will conquer. Well, almost. A good vision lives at about 50,000 feet. It does a good job of describing what the future state of the team or organization will look like after you're done, but it can be hard to really know what that will mean. Because this can lead to different people creating different concepts of success, it is important that you create a set of clear, objective, and ultimately measurable objectives. You need to set the expectation, with yourself, with your team, and within your management, that the effort will be judged based on these measurable objectives. This will be a useful tool in helping you understand where you are in your efforts and to protect you from subjective claims against them.

Define specific activities or improvements that are required to realize the objectives

At this point, you have almost all of the building blocks. Now you need to figure out what you actually need to accomplish. With the Vision and Objectives to guide you, identify specific actions that you can take that will move you toward your objectives. Write them down, assign them, and monitor their progress. To some degree, this is normal project management, but do not fall into the trap of just going through the motions. You are trying to build these five organizational traits and you need to keep laser-focused on that through the lens of your vision and objectives. If your activities are not moving you toward that vision, then stop, refocus, and begin again.

Communicate, communicate, communicate

As you begin this part of your journey, it is vital that people know what is going on. This is going to operate on three levels. First, much like the concept of 'going public' on your personal journey, by communicating to others that you and your team are going to begin this process, you will commit yourself to the effort much more clearly. Second, you need to ensure that you establish and maintain deep communication lines between you and others who are going through this process with you. The support of your team is critical, so it is essential that you communicate constantly and consistently with each other to keep everyone engaged. Finally, as you begin building these traits you will be impacting others in the organization, both positively and, potentially, negatively for a time. You need to let those impacted understand what you are doing and why you are doing it. People tend to be much more forgiving when they feel that they know what is going on. Do not leave anyone in the dark.

Rinse and repeat

Set yourself up for success. As you go down this road, make sure that you are initially selecting target areas that you have a reasonable opportunity to succeed in. Make sure that you build momentum and find success early. Once you do, you must continually reassess the situation and begin the process again. Developing these five traits will be a long process – you need to make sure that you are creating a repeatable life cycle that will enable you to sustain your development efforts.

THE QUANTUM AGE CONSORTIUM

As you begin your journey, there is one last resource that I would like to offer you. As I was writing this book, it occurred to me that it was only part of the story. This book describes what the future IT organization looks like, but in the form of traits and skills. There is a lot more to an organization than that. At the same time, IT executives and leaders at all levels do not have the luxury of living in a future world. You need to be able to connect this vision of the future of IT with the world that you are living in today.

You're not on this journey alone

As my partners and I thought about this, we realized that this was bigger than any one person or organization. More than that, it was going to take a lot of great minds to figure out how to create a framework that could connect the Quantum Age vision with the day-to-day reality that IT organizations are facing. Eventually, this developed into an idea to form what we chose to call the Quantum IT (or QIT) Consortium.

The QIT Consortium will represent an independent and diverse group of industry-thought leaders, IT executives, industry change agents, academics, and key representatives from consulting companies and tool suppliers working together to create a comprehensive framework for the IT organization of the future. Founded upon the principles set forth, this framework will establish a vision of how the IT organization of the near future will feel, operate, and interact with its customers. The Quantum IT Framework will also establish a roadmap that enables IT organizations to map tactical, short-term activities to the future-state vision.

The QIT Framework

The Quantum IT Framework represents both a vision for the operating traits and characteristics of the IT organization of the near future and a set of management tools that enables IT executives and leaders to simultaneously execute tactical activities while moving toward this vision. Unlike many of today's 'operational frameworks,' such as ITIL, COBIT, and IT-CMF, the QIT Framework will serve as a reference architecture for the fundamental makeup of the 'new' IT organization. The QIT Framework is founded on a series of core principles:

- The fundamental operating paradigm of the IT organization is shifting from a manufacturing model to a retail model.

- As the focus shifts from build and support to packaging and creating a customer experience, the organizational traits that make up the IT organization and the foundational skills of IT professionals must evolve.

- The evolution of these traits and skills will bring forth entirely new capability paradigms and organizational models that enable a new type of relationship between IT and its customer.

- The introduction of true competition means that IT organizations must complete this transformation at record speed in order to remain relevant.

- This transformation must be supported by both a strategic vision and tactical activities that enable the IT organization to operate effectively as it reshapes itself to meet the demands of the Quantum Age

When it is complete, the QIT Framework will serve as the roadmap allowing IT leaders to map their day-to-day activities to the broader Quantum Age vision. It will serve as a key building block on our journey to the future.

Join the movement

I would like to extend an invitation to you to join the QIT Consortium. We have created a website at *www.TheQuantumAgeofIT.com* to serve as the home for the consortium. As a member of the consortium, you will join a community of fellow IT professionals making the journey into the Quantum Age. You will be able to learn from them and exchange ideas as you endeavor to develop the five organizational traits and the five skills. You will also have the opportunity to be a part of developing the QIT Framework.

As a reader of this book, you will be given special privileges within the consortium. Simply enter the code 'QITBook' when registering to identify yourself as a reader.

We hope that you accept this invitation to join the consortium and be a part of the Quantum Age movement.

REFERENCES

The following books, journals, articles, white papers, other publications, and websites were used as reference during the production of this book.

Books

Ariely, Daniel. *Predictably Irrational: The Hidden Forces That Shape Our Decisions*, Harper, New York (2008)

Benioff, Marc and Adler, Carlyle. *Behind the Cloud: The Untold Story of How Salesforce.com Went from Idea to Billion-Dollar Company and Revolutionized an Industry*, John Wiley and Sons, San Francisco (2009), Kindle Edition

Birukoff, Paul. *The Life of Tolstoy*, Cassell & Co. Ltd, London (1911)

Christensen, Clayton M., Dyer, Jeff, and Gregersen, Hal. *The Innovator's DNA: Mastering the Five Skills of Disruptive Innovators*, Perseus Books Group (2011), Kindle Edition

Daft, Richard L. *Organization Theory and Design*, South-Western College Publishing (2006)

Godin, Seth. *Linchpin*, Penguin Group (2011)

Godin, Seth. *Tribes: We Need You to Lead Us*, Penguin Group (2008), Kindle Edition

Goldsmith, Marshall. *What Got You Here Won't Get You There*, Hyperion, New York (2007)

References

Grier, David Alan. *When Computers Were Human*. Princeton University Press, Princeton, NJ (2005)

Grimwood, Ken. *Replay*, William Morrow Paperbacks (1998)

Heath, Chip, and Heath, Dan. *Switch: How to Change Things When Change Is Hard*, Broadway Books, New York (2010)

Hogarth, Robin. *The Behavioral Foundations of Economic Theory* (1986)

Pink, Daniel. *Drive*, Penguin Group (2011)

Porter, Michael. *Comptetitive Advantage: Creating and Sustaining Superior Performance*, Free Press, New York (1985)

Rieger, Tom. *Breaking the Fear Barrier*, Gallup Press (2011)

Senge, Peter. *The Fifth Discipline*. Doubleday/Curency, New York (1990)

Sun Tzu. *The Art of War*. Oxford University Press, Oxford (1971)

Journals

Gamerer, Colin, Loewenstein, George, and Weber, Martin. "The Curse of Knowledge in Economic Settings: An Experimental Analysis." *Journal of Political Economy*, 97.5 (1989): pp. 1232–1254

Pollard, Sidney. "Factory Discipline in the Industrial Revolution." *Economic History Review*, New Series, 16.2 (1963): pp. 254–271

References

Treacy, Michael and Wiersema, Fred. "Customer Intimacy and Other Value Disciplines." *Harvard Business Review* (1993)

"Building with Big Data," *The Economist*, May 26, 2011

Online

Arzoomanian, Rich. "A Complete History of Mainframe Computing." *Tom's Hardware*. *http://www. tomshardware.com*. June 13, 2012

Butler, Jeremy G. "A History of Information Technology and Systems." University of Arizona, 1997. *http://www. tcf.ua.edu/AZ/ITHistoryOutline.htm*. Dec. 6, 2011

Canty, Monica. "Hotel Staff Must Be 'Empowered' to Solve Problems." *Hotelier MiddleEast*, Sept. 18, 2011. *http://www.hoteliermiddleeast.com*. June 13, 2012

Cheshire, Tom. "In Depth: How Rovio made Angry Birds a Winner (and What's Next)." *Wired*, Mar. 7, 2011. *http://www.wired.co.uk/magazine/archive/2011/04/features/ how-rovio-made-angry-birds-a-winner*. Dec. 6, 2011

Department of Computer Science at Virginia Tech. "The Machine That Changed the World." *Virginia Tech*, 1999. *http://ei.cs.vt.edu/~history/TMTCTW.html*. Dec. 6, 2011

Dwyer, Matt, Hatcliff, John, and Howell, Rod. "CIS 771: Software Specifications, Lecture 1: Course Overview." *Kansas State University*, 2001. *http://santos.cis.ksu. edu/771-Distribution/Slides/01-course-overview.pdf*. Dec. 6, 2011

References

Frost, Shawn. "Sun Tzu on Leadership." *Evan Carmichael.* *http://www.evancarmichael.com/Leadership/2044/Sun-Tzu-on-Leadership.html*. Jun. 3, 2012

Goldschmidt, Asaf and Akera, Atsushi. "The UNIVAC and the Legacy of the ENIAC." Department of History and Sociology of Science, University of Pennsylvania, 2003. *http://www.library.upenn.edu/exhibits/rbm/mauchly/jwm11.html*. Jun. 13, 2012

Grier, David Alan. "The Human Computer and the Birth of the Information Age." Philosophical Society of Washington, Washington State University, 2001. From the published version of the talk that appeared as "Human Computers: The First Pioneers of the Information Age." *Endeavor* 25.1 (March 2001), pp. 28–32. *http://www.philsoc.org/2001Spring/2132transcript.html*. Nov. 8, 2011

Heath, Chip and Heath, Dan. "The Curse of Knowledge." *Harvard Business Review*, Dec. 2006. *http://hbr.org/2006/12/the-curse-of-knowledge/ar*. Nov. 2, 2011

Hylton, Wil S. "What Happened to Air France Flight 447?" *New York Times Magazine*, 4 May 2011. *http://www.nytimes.com/2011/05/08/magazine/mag-08Plane-t.html?_r=1&pagewanted=all*. Jun. 2, 2012

Robison, Jennifer. "How the Ritz-Carlton Manages the Mystique." *Gallup Business Journal.* *http://businessjournal.gallup.com/content/112906/How-RitzCarlton-Manages-Mystique.aspx*. Jun. 13, 2012

Rubin, Courtney. "Internet Users over Age 50 Flocking to Social Media." *Inc. Magazine*, 30 Aug. 2010. *http://www.inc.com/news/articles/2010/08/users-over-50-*

References

are-fastest-growing-social-media-demographic.html. Jun. 13, 2012

Rugaber, Christopher S. "Old Skills, Not Enough to Aid Jobless." *Akron Beacon Journal Online,* Jun. 18, 2011. *http://www.ohio.com.* May, 30 2012

Russell, Eric. "LePage: Plenty of Jobs, Not Enough Skills." *Bangor Daily News,* Sept. 9, 2011. *http://bangordailynews.com.* May 30, 2012

Schumpeter Blog. "Building with Big Data." *The Economist,* Mar. 26, 2011. *http://bangordailynews.com.* Jun. 13, 2012

Tolstoy, Leo. "The Three Questions." *The Literature Network.* *http://www.online-literature.com/tolstoy/2736.* May 30, 2012

Trent Hamm. "Review: What You Got Won't Get You There." *The Simple Dollar,* Dec. 7, 2007. *http://www.thesimpledollar.com/2007/12/02/review-what-got-you-here-wont-get-you-there.* May 30, 2012

"Bankers Tout Mobile-Capture Success, Warn Others to Jump in Soon." *Digital Transactions,* Mar. 8, 2011. *http://digitaltransactions.net/news/story/2962.* Jun. 13, 2012

"Columbus Ships Crew." *http://www.christopher-columbus.eu/ships-crew.htm.* Jun. 4, 2012

"Early FedEx History." *FedEx Legends.* *http://www.fedexlegends.info.* Jun. 14, 2012

"FedEx Innovations." *FedEx.* *http://about.van.fedex.com/company-information.* Jun. 14, 2012

References

"Google Achieves Significant Business, Growth Milestones in 2000." *Google*, 1 Feb. 2001. *http://www.google.com/intl/en/press/pressrel/pressrelease5 1.html*. Jun. 13, 2012

"Google Annual Search Statistics." *Statistics Brain*, Mar 14, 2012. *http://www.statisticbrain.com/google-searches*. Jun. 13, 2012

"Google Company Overview." *Google*. *http://www. google.com/intl/en/about/company*. Jan. 24, 2012

"Legendary Steve Jobs Quotes." *The Exception Magazine*, Oct 6, 2011. *http://exceptionmag.com*. May 29, 2012

"Malcolm Gladwell on Spaghetti Sauce." *TED.com*, 2004. *http://www.ted.com*. May 29, 2012

"Our History in Depth." *Google*. *http://www.google.com/ about/company/history*. Dec. 6, 2011

"Ray Kroc." *Answers.com*. *http://www.answers.com/ topic/ray-kroc*. Mar. 9, 2012

"The Three Questions." *Wikipedia*. *http://en.wikipedia. org/wiki/The_Three_Questions*. May 30, 2012

"Top 10 Famous Expeditions." *TopTenz.net*. *http://www. toptenz.net/top-10-famous-expeditions.php*. Jun. 4, 2012

"United States Facebook Statistics." *SocialBakers.com*. *http://www.socialbakers.com/facebook-statistics/united-states*. Jun. 13, 2012

Interviews

Lefebvre, Mojgan. Personal interview. Dec. 12, 2011.

Manfredo, Joel. Personal interview. Jul. 25, 2011.

References

Pleasant, Joe. Personal interview. Nov. 28, 2011.

Rangan, Ashwin. Personal interview. Jul. 27, 2011.

Scott, Geoff. Personal interview. Oct. 5, 2011.

Wray, Bill. Personal interview. Jul. 20, 2011.

ITG RESOURCES

IT Governance Ltd. sources, creates and delivers products and services to meet the real-world, evolving IT governance needs of today's organisations, directors, managers and practitioners.

The ITG website (_www.itgovernance.co.uk_) is the international one-stop-shop for corporate and IT governance information, advice, guidance, books, tools, training and consultancy.

Other Websites

Books and tools published by IT Governance Publishing (ITGP) are available from all business booksellers and are also immediately available from the following websites:

http://www.itgovernance.eu is our euro-denominated website which ships from Benelux and has a growing range of books in European languages other than English.

www.itgovernanceusa.com is a US$-based website that delivers the full range of IT Governance products to North America, and ships from within the continental US.

www.itgovernanceasia.com provides a selected range of ITGP products specifically for customers in the Indian sub-continent.

www.itgovernance.asia delivers the full range of ITGP publications, serving countries across Asia Pacific. Shipping from Hong Kong, US dollars, Singapore dollars, Hong Kong dollars, New Zealand dollars and Thai baht are all accepted through the website.

www.27001.com is the IT Governance Ltd website that deals specifically with information security management, and ships from within the continental US.

Toolkits

ITG's unique range of toolkits includes the IT Governance Framework Toolkit, which contains all the tools and guidance that you will need in order to develop and implement an appropriate IT governance framework for your organisation. Full details can be found at *www.itgovernance.co.uk/ products/519*.

For a free paper on how to use the proprietary Calder-Moir IT Governance Framework, and for a free trial version of the toolkit, see *www.itgovernance.co.uk/calder_moir.aspx*.

There is also a wide range of toolkits to simplify implementation of management systems, such as an ISO/IEC 27001 ISMS or an ISO/IEC 22301 BCMS, and these can all be viewed and purchased online at: *http://www.itgovernance.co.uk/catalog/1*.

Training Services

IT Governance offers an extensive portfolio of training courses designed to educate information security, IT governance, risk management and compliance professionals. Our classroom and online training programmes will help you develop the skills required to deliver best practice and compliance to your organisation. They will also enhance your career by providing you with industry-standard certifications and increased peer recognition. Our range of courses offers a structured learning path from foundation to advanced level in the key topics of information security, IT governance, business continuity and service management.

Full details of all IT Governance training courses can be found at *http://www.itgovernance.co.uk/training.aspx*.

Professional Services and Consultancy

IT Governance standards compliance/management systems consultants have years of experience, ensuring that our clients can benefit from the 'Quantum Age' of Internet technologies.

Our consultancy services assist you in managing Internet service strategies in harmony with business goals, conveying the right messages to colleagues to supporting decision making.

We expertly guide you in designing and implementing policies, procedures and controls that help your company to become:

• A Learning Organisation

• A Disciplined Organisation

• A Transparent Organisation

• An Intimate Organisation

• A Dynamic Organisation.

In particular, we can show you how to develop information security management systems (ISMS) to fully comply with the growing ISO27001 Standard; to protect your data, maintain its integrity and make it easily available to everyone who needs it within your organisation, whenever and wherever it's required.

For more information about IT Governance Consultancy services, see *http://www.itgovernance.co.uk/consulting.aspx*.

Publishing Services

IT Governance Publishing (ITGP) is the world's leading IT-GRC publishing imprint that is wholly owned by IT Governance Ltd.

ITG Resources

With books and tools covering all IT governance, risk and compliance frameworks, we are the publisher of choice for authors and distributors alike, producing unique and practical publications of the highest quality, in the latest formats available, which readers will find invaluable.

www.itgovernancepublishing.co.uk is the website dedicated to ITGP, enabling both current and future authors, distributors, readers and other interested parties to have easier access to more information, allowing them to keep up to date with the latest publications and news from ITGP.

Newsletter

IT governance is one of the hottest topics in business today, not least because it is also the fastest-moving.

You can stay up to date with the latest developments across the whole spectrum of IT governance subject matter, including risk management, information security, ITIL and IT service management, project governance, compliance and so much more, by subscribing to ITG's core publications and topic alert emails.

Simply visit our subscription centre and select your preferences: *www.itgovernance.co.uk/newsletter.aspx*.